Danny Boyle: Interviews

Conversations with Filmmakers Series
Gerald Peary, General Editor

Danny Boyle
INTERVIEWS

Edited by Brent Dunham

University Press of Mississippi / Jackson

www.upress.state.ms.us

The University Press of Mississippi is a member of the Association of American University Presses.

Copyright © 2011 by University Press of Mississippi
All rights reserved
Manufactured in the United States of America

First printing 2011
∞
Library of Congress Cataloging-in-Publication Data

Boyle, Danny.
   Danny Boyle : interviews / edited by Brent Dunham.
      p. cm. — (Conversations with filmmakers series)
   Includes filmography and index.
   ISBN 978-1-60473-833-9 (cloth : alk. paper) — ISBN 978-1-60473-834-6 (pbk. : alk. paper) — ISBN 978-1-60473-835-3 (ebook) — ISBN 978-1-4968-5797-2 (paperback)
1. Boyle, Danny—Interviews. 2. Motion picture
producers and directors—Great Britain—Interviews. I. Dunham, Brent. II. Title.
   PN1998.3.B685A3 2011
   791.430'28092—dc22
   [B]   2010029816

British Library Cataloging-in-Publication Data available

Contents

Introduction

"Everyone was saying my dad will be able to graze sheep on his lawn now!"[1] After winning an Oscar for Best Director, most people would imagine this success to provide a little more benefit than giving your father unprecedented grazing rights but, then again, not everyone is Danny Boyle. Perhaps as philosophically and creatively far away from Hollywood as a mainstream filmmaker can be, Danny Boyle has made a cinematic career out of bending the rules, ignoring expectations, and, frankly, going unnoticed for the past decade. That is, until now. *Slumdog Millionaire*, released in 2008, became Danny Boyle's crowning achievement. Winning eight Oscars out of ten nominations, seven BAFTAs out of eleven nominations and all four Golden Globes it was nominated for, the film was a textbook hit, the kind of undeniable phenomenon that most directors never achieve. And yet, this working-class Briton of Irish descent did the impossible: he brought a starless "foreign film" that almost died in "straight to DVD hell" into worldwide attention and appreciation.

Though his film career spans only fifteen years, Boyle's journey has been a lot longer. He discovered an interest in drama while attending the University of Bangor in Wales but, as he describes, jumping straight into filmmaking was a tad far-fetched. "I couldn't get into the British film industry because it was very fenced off at the time, very clubby."[2] Theatre, as it turns out, was much more accepting of the newcomer. Working in various capacities for the Joint Stock Theatre Company and the Royal Court Theatre Upstairs, Boyle then took another step closer to Hollywood by taking a job in television no one else wanted. In 1987, he began producing programs for BBC Northern Ireland when "The Troubles" there still had a decade of violence and tension left to go. In 1994, Boyle and his team, consisting of producer Andrew Macdonald and screenwriter John Hodge, took *Shallow Grave*, their first feature film, to Cannes where popular demand forced organizers to schedule additional screenings. This was just the beginning.

When considering the function of a collection of interviews, it becomes clear that there is no unified theory on how to present every artist. In a sense, the artist dictates how he or she will be presented and understood by their audiences and critics. As individualistic and varied as artists can be, it follows that their reception would be equally diverse. If you've ever read an interview with David Lynch, you know that he can be as maddeningly vague as his films. If you've ever seen a Lars von Trier film, you might not be surprised when his dealings with the press are fittingly controversial. Some filmmakers, most notoriously Hitchcock, use the interview to cultivate and promote a personal mythology. The question is: how shall Danny Boyle be presented? Or, more accurately, how has Danny Boyle allowed himself to be presented?

As a filmmaker, Danny Boyle is an interesting specimen. There is a spectrum of popular filmmakers that ranges from the completely commercial to the completely artistic. Some directors are content to get handed assignments from Hollywood studios as directors for hire, while others are fiercely independent and wholly focused on pushing the boundaries of what popular cinema can be. Directly in the middle of these two extremes is Boyle, and *Slumdog Millionaire* becomes the perfect example to illustrate this point: the film is populist enough to be dubbed "the feel-good movie of the year" while simultaneously stretching what's acceptable for mainstream audiences. This is not the first film to strike this delicate balance, and Boyle is not the first filmmaker to embrace this philosophy. What makes him peculiar is his nonchalance, his lack of personal agenda, his humility to admit when he's wrong, and his polite acceptance of accolades. As journalist Brian Libby noted, "For all his talents, perhaps the best thing you can say about Boyle is that he's still just an unassuming lad."[3] In an industry of egos and corporations, of agents and politics, we find a man making films that resonate across genre and demographics, an artist who refuses to let his vision supersede the story, and we find a success story who hasn't forgotten where he came from.

One important trend to point out, a characteristic that will carry throughout his career, is his devotion to cinema as a venue for entertainment first, art second. Besides a recent textual analysis by author Edwin Page,[4] Boyle and his films have yet to be considered seriously in academic or critical spheres and perhaps this personal philosophy is responsible. Additionally, even from this humble beginning, Boyle proudly positions himself as a "business-conscious director" when so many emerging filmmakers seem fixated on making a significant artistic splash. "Cinema is a popular medium," insists Boyle. "We have to make more idiosyncratic films, but that needn't eschew popularity."[5] And, upon consideration of this first film and those that followed, we can see that Boyle has attempted this feat at every opportunity.

As far as influence and inspiration are concerned, Danny Boyle won't be the one to give you a laundry list of cinematic icons. We know from these interviews that seeing *A Clockwork Orange* during its limited release in Britain was an inspiring moment, and we also know that *Apocalypse Now* is his favorite film. He claims to have aped Scorsese's style on *Trainspotting*, but that comparison won't hold water for everyone. No, Boyle even admits that the real inspiration is his love for music. Growing up near Manchester, his ties to the city's veritable wellspring of talent has made its mark upon him. In his own words: "My biggest influence is music. That's my biggest single influence and I'm proud to come from an area where the music scene and the rock stars it produces are unbelievable."[6] One needn't look any further than *Trainspotting*: the opening scene itself instantly became one of those great moments of cinema, and it can be said that the thumping Iggy Pop song made it so. The film's soundtrack became a phenomenon in itself, prompting not one but *two* albums worth of music, and it landed number seven on *Vanity Fair's* "Greatest Movie Soundtracks." Simon Hattenstone put Boyle's obsession with music very succinctly when he said, "At times the characters seem like a backdrop to the soundtrack."[7] Boyle is constantly attempting to give his films a certain vibrancy and vivacity, and, to achieve this, music often becomes one of his most effective tools.

As an interviewee, Danny Boyle comes off as gracious, accommodating, and genuine. While some directors, such as the Coen Brothers, use the few interviews they grant as a platform to emphasize their playful, sarcastic, and non-participatory reputation, Boyle conducts each interview like it's his first, answering questions consistently and thoroughly, showing endless enthusiasm for his work, and giving respect and consideration to the interviewer with little ego, elitism, or jaded distrust of the media. Even when a majority of his post-*Trainspotting* interviews inquire about a sequel to that film, and even after he gives the same answer every time, Boyle never seems to be bothered by it. Some artists become plagued by their earlier successes as fans and critics simply want "another *Trainspotting*"; Boyle acknowledges why this question would be asked over and over without conceding to replicate his work in future projects. In fact, Boyle doesn't even allow himself to believe that he will be around long enough to make said sequel. Even after garnering the top awards in the film industry, if his career was suddenly over, he probably wouldn't be surprised. He'd simply chalk it up to having his fifteen minutes, which is more than most people ever get.

Many of the early interviews focus on the relationship between Boyle and co-conspirators Macdonald and Hodge. Some even include them in the interview process, furthering the notion that they function as an entity greater than the sum of its parts. After *The Beach* when they essentially went their separate ways, the focus remains on Boyle and his current collaborators, such as writer Alex Garland or actor Cillian Murphy. Because he's easily one of the least controversial filmmakers, Boyle is rarely asked about his personal life. The closest we come to relating the man to his work is during the interviews pertaining to *Millions*, where there is actually more of a connection between the artist and the material.

Therefore, as this collection shows, the majority of questions are aimed at the filmmaking process. Certainly, many set pieces in Boyle's films would spark the question in even the most passive film-goers: "How did you do that?" Presenting scenes and images we can't easily find in real life has always been part of the appeal of cinema and, ever-conscious of the audience, Boyle excels at this. How does one go about emptying the streets of London for *28 Days Later . . .* ? What is it like filming in the slums of Mumbai? How did you film Ewan McGregor crawling inside a toilet? This is not to say that Boyle's films are all style and no substance, nor do the interviewers ever appear to treat them as such. Depending on the interviewer, deeper issues and/or connections are addressed: the responsibility of the artist and the portrayal of drug use, ideas of faith and its relationship to youth, *Shallow Grave* as a cultural reflection of early nineties' Britain, or the impetus behind *28 Days Later . . .* as a symptom of the twenty-first century. Instead of taking the long way around these issues or overly complicating them with pretentious jargon, Boyle is fully aware of their relevance and tends to handle his responses with clarity and thoughtfulness.

Humility has been a part of Danny Boyle's persona from the very beginning, but when one considers some of his interests and activities outside making movies, it appears to be the real deal. Most recently, Boyle and Christian Colson, his producer on *Slumdog Millionaire,* quelled accusations of exploiting that film's young stars by setting up trust funds in their names. Critics in India and elsewhere denounced the film for its portrayal of these lower-class citizens, but the only condition given to the children was that they had to remain in school and complete their education before they'd see any of the money. While this was perhaps the most public display of humanitarianism from Danny Boyle, it certainly wasn't the first. In 2004, he wrote a piece on the "eco-cide" and the resulting poverty taking place in Muynak, Uzbekistan, for the *Sunday Times.*[8] As part of the "Authors in the Front Line" series, Boyle exhibits a recognizable kind of compassion and concern for those furthest away from red carpets and flashing cameras. In 2005, Boyle began his work on the Board of Trustees for Dramatic Need, a U.K.-based charity that supports arts programs for underprivileged children in South Africa. In November 2008, Boyle wrote an article for the *Times* about Dramatic Need, including profiles on some individual beneficiaries of the program.[9] "Through the arts, young children living in catastrophic circumstances need to be given something to live for and something through which to express their lives."[10]

An honest attempt has been made here to present Danny Boyle's career through interviews, giving equal attention to both the popular and lesser-known films. It's been said that one can learn more from watching terrible movies than from watching classics, and, following this logic, perhaps we learn more about filmmakers themselves through their mistakes, ill-fated films, and moments of vulnerability. We don't have such extreme lows here because even though Boyle has had a couple misfires, they weren't so dramatic as to end his career. Then there's the fact that we end the collection on such a high note after *Slumdog Millionaire*'s amazing success, making Boyle himself look like Dev Patel's character, Jamal, from the film: a true underdog. The articles/interviews have been selected based on two criteria: the quality of their writing and questions and their ability to construct a consistent and thorough path through the fifteen years of Boyle's career. Admittedly, the amount of choices for interviews for *Shallow Grave* as opposed to *Slumdog Millionaire* is understandably limited; there's quite a bit of difference between a first-time filmmaker touring festivals with a low-budget indie and a Best Picture winner. For the most part, each feature film in Boyle's oeuvre, ten and counting, is equally represented throughout the collection. There is even an article specifically dedicated to the transitional period Boyle entered after *The Beach*, centered on the two television films he directed for the BBC. The variety of sources included in this collection provides similarly various perspectives, both from the questions being asked and from the answers given. We have here pieces from major newspapers, academic journals, a post-screening Q&A session, independent film blogs, a film school interview, a transcript from a talk-show appearance, and on-location interviews. Through these various mediums and venues, a more thorough examination of Danny Boyle as a filmmaker and as an individual can be achieved.

This collection begins with Danny Boyle talking about his first feature film, *Shallow Grave*. The discussion between Boyle and writer Ronan Bennett covers some lofty topics such as the purpose of narrative, strategies of characterization, and the responsibilities of an artist. Boyle handles himself deftly through this intellectual minefield, which may seem surprising since *Shallow Grave* is his first "proper" feature film but, then again, not many first-time directors these days spent more than a decade directing theatre and television beforehand. For example, when asked about the role of detailed characterization, Boyle rejects the idea that it is a priority for audiences watching the film. "[T]he problem with traditional character development is that audiences are not there primarily to watch a character being drawn. What they want is the excitement and the speed of the journey that cinema can provide."[11] So, already, Boyle is acutely aware of the differences between the visual mediums he's been working with. What works for theatre may not work for television, which, in turn, may not work for cinema. "What you learn in television is not really relevant to the cinema—you'd think it would be—but the sense of scale is completely different."[12] His experiences prior to feature filmmaking have obviously given him a "head start" on so many beginning filmmakers, especially contemporary directors, as his trial-and-error period went essentially unnoticed by critics and audiences outside Britain's theatre and television circles.

Shallow Grave was indeed a relatively critical and commercial success. When it debuted out of competition at Cannes in 1994, positive reactions turned into additional screenings, and it went on to win a BAFTA for Best British Film and Boyle was named British Newcomer of the Year at the London Critics Circle Film Awards. For all his success with *Shallow Grave*, it would be his next film, *Trainspotting*, to solidify his position as a savior of British cinema. In 1996, Boyle brought Irvine Welsh's dystopian novel about heroin addicts in Edinburgh to life with help from the usual suspects: producer Andrew Macdonald, screen-writer John Hodge, and actor Ewan McGregor. If *Shallow Grave* can be called a "hit" in relative terms, *Trainspotting* was a phenomenon. The film was a sensation in and out of Britain and became one of the most iconic films of the 1990s. Hodge's script went on to win a BAFTA and was nominated for an Academy Award. The Empire Awards in the U.K. awarded Boyle Best Director, Ewan McGregor Best Actor, Ewen Bremner Best Debut, and the film itself Best Picture. *Los Angeles Times* critic Kenneth Turan begins his review with "Exuberant and pitiless, profane yet eloquent, flush with the ability to create laughter out of unspeakable situations, *Trainspotting* is a drop-dead look at a dead-end lifestyle that has all the strength of its considerable contradictions."[13] The film generated controversy not simply for portraying drug use but for making it look "fun." During the 1996 presidential elections, Senator Bob Dole singled the film out for its potentially corrosive effect upon society. Undeterred, the film drew people from all walks of life in to a new, darker side of Scotland, and *Rolling Stone*'s Peter Travers summed it up best: "*Braveheart* it ain't."[14]

At that point, Boyle had two hits in a row but still only those two films under his belt. This leaves little room for the interviews to explore many comparisons between this and other works, but since *Trainspotting* does indeed appear to be cut from the same cloth as *Shallow Grave*, comparisons can be (and are) made. Keith Hopper posits that it is the low budgets that incite the stylistic choices in the films, and Boyle fully acknowledges this. "With any low-budget film, aesthetic considerations are inseparable from budgetary ones."[15] Stylistically, both films are clearly related, but it is the subject matter of *Trainspotting* that draws the most attention. While *Shallow Grave*'s theme centers on murder, perhaps a more familiar or old-fashioned premise, *Trainspotting*'s treatment of heroin use is a much pricklier situation. With obviously careful consideration, Boyle offers his approach: "I don't think that you can preach to people about drugs in the modern world, it's pointless . . . and you can't patronize them by claiming that you know better. All you're doing by that is alienating them, and satisfying a much older generation who need the comfort of knowing that drugs are being condemned."[16]

Shallow Grave and *Trainspotting* were a veritable "1-2-punch," two films that not only signaled a rebirth for the U.K. film industry but the arrival of a new talent in Danny Boyle and his team. The future was bright as their next project set the stage for further upward mobility and a wider palette. "Then," as Brian Libby puts it, "Boyle promptly lost his way."[17] *A Life Less Ordinary*, which starred Ewan McGregor and Cameron Diaz, ultimately became the first of two misfires in a row. Set and shot in America with a mostly American cast, this quirky romantic comedy was meant to be their proper introduction to the U.S. market, but Boyle's "junior (not sophomore) slump" confused critics and audiences alike with an eccentric plot populated with eccentric characters. Critically, it was smashed, but Boyle still claims he has a special place for *A Life Less Ordinary* as one of his favorites. In his piece, Ben Thompson acknowledges the film's shortcomings and addresses them in the interview along with suggestions that the "team" was having difficulty with this latest, not-as-warmly-embraced film. There is a sense here that Boyle realizes these faults and is willing to accept them but he's also in the process of promoting the film, and so he walks a fine line. "Looking at the film now, I think one of the good things about it is that it is slightly free-form. If people get caught up in it, they will enjoy the fact that some of it is pretty inexplicable—not in the way a David Lynch film would be, because it's lighter than that—but it is quite free. And the justification for that, and this is the pompous bit, is that that's a bit like what it's like to be in love." While the film was a disappointment, Boyle and his team not only stayed in Hollywood, their next film, *The Beach*, would be the largest-scale film they had yet to attempt.

Boyle's film career can be divided into two eras: the initial explosion onto the scene and his most recent renaissance. The dividing point comes directly after *The Beach*. Boyle, Macdonald, and Hodge went bigger with this project: their budget was significantly higher than all three of their previous films combined, they had Leonardo DiCaprio (the biggest star on the planet at the time) in the lead role, and they filmed on location in Thailand. These heightened circumstances can be read as a natural progression from the dregs of independent filmmaking into the professionalism of the Hollywood system, but it ended becoming an expensive lesson for Boyle to realize he was not cut out for this type of directing. It's not that he felt he wasn't talented enough or incapable of working in the Hollywood machine; he simply realized he was at his best working on a lower scale: "I've decided not to do those big-budget films. I don't think I'm very good at them."[18] Boyle admits that *The Beach* was a product of an attempt to expand their work, to broaden their horizons and push themselves further than they'd been. The fact that Leonardo DiCaprio was cast instead of Ewan McGregor (even though there was apparently a verbal agreement that McGregor had the job) has been questioned as a purely financial decision, but Boyle claims it had more to do with challenging himself as an artist: "People have said to me that using Leo was just playing for the dollar. Well, if I wanted to take the least risk possible, I'd have made *Trainspotting 2*. I've been asked often enough. *The Beach* with Ewan McGregor would have been too easy."[19] The film was adapted from a novel by Alex Garland who would later become a frequent collaborator as screenwriter for *28 Days Later . . .* and *Sunshine*. On a $50 million budget, the film only brought in $39 million domestically and was dismissed by the critics. Even though it was considered a bomb, it still made $104 million more internationally.[20] Tom Charity's conversation with Boyle, Macdonald, Hodge, and Garland precedes the film's release and is therefore able to focus on more typical topics: themes present in the film such as urban dissatisfaction and escape to paradise, the changes made from book to film, and the process of turning a bleak novel into a mainstream, studio film. Describing this relationship, Boyle has this to say, "For [Hollywood studios], a film has to be a journey of redemption, ultimately. They'll take any kind of darkness if it's got a hokey happy ending; they're mad about 'completion,' for characters and for stories."[21] In spite of their honest attempts to make the film more palatable (Boyle actually preferred the film's new ending to the book's), it failed to meet expectations, but it taught Boyle a valuable lesson which has shaped his career ever since: stay away from Hollywood.

After licking his wounds from *The Beach*, Boyle applied what he learned from the experience and brought himself back down to more familiar and comfortable territory: television. As Dennis Lim puts it, "Instead of hanging around Hollywood waiting for his shot at redemption,"[22] he went back to England and in 2001 he made two features for the BBC, *Strumpet* and *Vacuuming Completely Nude in Paradise*. Instead of former team member John Hodge, the scripts for both films were written by Jim Cartwright, an old associate of Boyle's from his theatre days. This also marks the first time Boyle experimented with digital video, and he enlisted one of the most respected artists working in the medium, Anthony Dod Mantle. An Englishman who lives in Denmark, Dod Mantle perfected his video techniques working with cinema's petulant child, Lars von Trier, and the rest of the Dogme 95 brethren on their stripped-down, artifice-allergic films. For the first time, Danny

Boyle was operating without his team. Writing for the *Guardian*, Simon Hattenstone uses the term "BHM movie" (**B**oyle/**H**odge/**M**acdonald) to describe the trio's films as collective artistic endeavors. What then would happen when a "BHM movie" was reduced to "B movie"? The separation was amicable, Macdonald returned to produce *28 Days Later* . . . and *Sunshine*, and Hodge is reportedly working on the prophesized *Trainspotting* sequel, but it also allowed Boyle to begin anew. Working in a different medium, with a new writer, and now free from the pressure that was *The Beach*, the second era of Danny Boyle's career would begin small and simple. As he relates to Rupert Smith here, he was consciously looking for a change. "The entire budget for these two films [*Vacuuming* and *Strumpet*] would barely have covered the catering on *The Beach*. I had a desire to do something that would open out the way I work, that would be more spontaneous."

Working on video for his two BBC films, Boyle found the medium to be liberating. In the still relevant debate over "film vs. digital," he hasn't completely forsaken celluloid, and he also hasn't turned into a digital video evangelist. Boyle recognizes both the benefits of the two mediums, their inherent qualities that lend themselves to specific narratives, and that the choice of which to use on a given film must be genuinely motivated. It just so happens that his next project, *28 Days Later* . . . , fit like a glove with the aesthetic qualities of DV. Working again with Anthony Dod Mantle, Boyle brought himself back to feature filmmaking with a new lead actor and a new genre. In fact, after his previous projects consistently avoid categorization, the film was the first time Boyle has committed himself to an actual genre film. Both Boyle and screenwriter Alex Garland acknowledge their indebtedness to the groundwork laid by zombie film icon George A. Romero and author John Wyndham's *The Day of the Triffids*, but they object to calling it a zombie film: "It's not a film about monsters—it's a film about us!"[23] The film was a financial and critical success: made for $8 million, it returned $82 million in world-wide gross, and yet it had no recognizable stars, a low budget, and was shot on video in England. Saying Boyle went "back to his roots" would not only be a cliché, but it would also be a reductive assessment of his achievement. This was new territory for him and it would begin Boyle's second successful run. The fact that *28 Days Later* . . . was unlike anything he'd done previously suggests that Boyle emerged from his short but fruitful hiatus a stronger and more confident artist. Later, Boyle would make *Sunshine*, a sci-fi thriller, again switching generic gears and prompting Dennis Lim to call Boyle a "professional chameleon,"[24] describing his ability to graft himself onto various narratives and genres.

The interviews associated with *28 Days Later . . .* cover various topics such as the obvious influences and precedents to the film ("We were not stealing, but nothing can stand on its own anymore—there is always some reference point."[25]), the connections between the blood-transmitted virus in the film to AIDS and more contemporary biological concerns such as anthrax and SARS, and the film's progressive use of DV. To Sandy Hunter, Boyle justified his use of digital video in a particularly thoughtful way: "We wanted it to feel different in texture from normal film. Because it's an apocalypse, you can use a different hue, because nobody knows what things will look like if everybody's killed or there are no cars."[26] Despite Boyle's dedication to entertainment, his films are often populated with strong ideas and cultural reflections. In this, his contribution to a subgenre typically considered empty of value, we find a modern parable, thinly veiled as a horror film and a distinct product of the post-modern experience. "It's been a crucial part of the last two decades of British life, with the individual dominating in a way society can't sustain. [W]e sell these dreams to people so brilliantly now that we are far ahead of our capability of delivering them, so people become obsessed . . . You get tension, frustration builds and violence comes in. Those are ideas we worked with."[27] The film was in the middle of production on September 11, 2001, making the imagery and iconography almost too relevant for the filmmakers, but when considering editing out potentially sensitive material, producer Andrew Macdonald says, "This is what raises the film from being just a genre movie."[28]

Following the dark, bloody, and hellish apocalypse of *28 Days Later . . .* , Danny Boyle jumped into a genre many people wouldn't think possible: the family film. Released in 2005, *Millions* is perhaps his most personal film to date. The film revolves around two young brothers who find a giant bag of money, British pounds to be exact, and they have to decide how to spend it all before England's fictionalized switch over to the Euro. The lead character, Damien (Alex Etel), isn't necessarily deeply religious but he spends most of his time in dialogue with various Saints as his imaginary friends. The strong religious themes and visions are an homage to his parents, especially his mother, and Boyle dedicated the film to them. Boyle grew up in an Irish Catholic household, spearheaded by his mother whose wish was for her son to become a priest. It almost happened, too, until an actual priest talked him out of it. The film isn't strictly anchored in religion; it owes most of its philosophy to faith and the innocence of youth. Damien, young enough to not yet be tainted by greed, wants to use this new-found money to help others rather than himself.

During this period, perhaps for the first time, Boyle had a chance to take a break from explaining the formal strategies of filmmaking and discuss more meaningful and personal topics such as his relationship with his parents, his thoughts on youth and faith, and the liberating experience of working with child actors. To Brendan MacDevette, Boyle explains that even though the most obvious or simple theme to *Millions* is religious faith, the central conceit is more complex. "It is not a strictly religious sensibility, it has more to do with having faith in people and that goodness can come out of that."[29] To Jeffrey Overstreet, Boyle expands on this idea: "It's faith that's linked to the imagination—the power of taking a leap—rather than it being faith in a strictly conventional religious sense."[30] Such a concept might seem a daunting task to pull off without seeming disingenuous or unnatural, but that's exactly why Boyle used children and their imagination through which to frame the story. Another observation often made is the connection *Millions* has to his first film, *Shallow Grave*, as the catalyst for both narratives come in the form of a large bag of money. Despite their similarities, Boyle explains that both films are actually indicative of the transition Britain's made in between. "I think it shows the differences in England when each movie was made. The first movie was made in a cynical period when there was a Gordon Gekko, 'greed is good' mentality prevalent. The second, made in the Tony Blair era, reflects the Labor Party trying to do good in the country. It felt like a different era in Britain."[31] *Millions* was not much of a commercial success (one reason, perhaps, was its limited release), but critics embraced the film. Roger Ebert named it one of the top ten films of 2005 and had this to say about it: "Here is a film that exists in that enchanted realm where everything goes right—not for the characters, for the filmmakers. They take an enormous risk with a film of sophistication and whimsy, about children, money, criminals, and saints."[32] Perhaps this critical encouragement is what allowed Boyle to take his next project where he previously feared to tread: outer space.

During the mid-nineties, after the major success of *Trainspotting*, Boyle was offered the chance to direct the fourth installment of the

Alien series. After some consideration, he turned it down. "I didn't know what I was doing, and I wouldn't have known how to handle all the special effects that would have been a huge part of it. So I backed out of it."[33] Ten years later, Boyle did eventually make his way back to the sci-fi genre with more confidence in himself and in the advanced technology. Written by Alex Garland, *Sunshine* was yet again a significant transition in tone, style, and genre. It also required the biggest budget Boyle had worked with since *The Beach*, but the circumstances alone suggest that this time around he'd be working on his own terms. The film was shot in London with a seasoned, international cast but even as a big-budget sci-fi film, it still had that "lack of Hollywood" that Boyle has made work ever since he went frolicking with Leonardo in Thailand. Cillian Murphy, an unknown when he starred in *28 Days Later* . . . , returns with a bit more clout: he made both critical and commercial waves in films like *Batman Begins, Red Eye, Breakfast on Pluto,* and *The Wind That Shakes the Barley*. Financially, the film did not do well at the box office, bringing in a dismal $3 million domestically, but to its credit, according to Box Office Mojo, the film's widest U.S. release was only 461 theaters. When discussing *Sunshine*, it is obvious that the film challenged Danny Boyle; he acknowledges both the benefits of such a challenge and his desire to never do it again. When asked by Kevin Polowy which genre he would never work in, Boyle quickly responds, "Space movies. Never again."[34] Like the precedents set before his other genre film, *28 Days Later* . . . , Boyle explains the pressure of working in the shadow of the great films like *2001: A Space Odyssey* and *Alien* and the overwhelming task of putting his own stamp upon the genre. "The demands of getting to that level that's been set by all those predecessor films is really tough, and you don't realize how tough it is until you start trying to do that stuff: weightlessness, the isolation, lack of anything to cut to . . ."[35] As *Sunshine* was Boyle's first heavily CG-based film, many topics discussed here inevitably focus on formal techniques and working with an ensemble cast in such confined quarters. One topic that arises not only sheds some light on Boyle's approach to *Sunshine*, but we can see that same philosophy throughout his career: working with extremes. To Amber Wilkinson, Boyle describes his predilection for extremes, whether they be genres, characterizations, themes, or visual design. "Always try to accentuate extremes if you can. [*Trainspotting*] could have been a more neutral film, a slightly more boring film. But we took a risk in making it extremely funny and extremely disturbing—and one bashes up against the next one. It's very risky, but I love doing that." For *Sunshine* specifically, he explains that the two extremes utilized is both the beauty and the violence inherent in space; the calm, cool interiors of the spaceship clashing head-on with the enormous ferocity of the Sun. "People don't just go to the cinema anymore . . . So to make that cinema, that big event, it should be as much like a car crash as possible. Extremes of beauty and violence."[36] Certainly, working with extremes was a requisite for his next project, the project that would change everything.

His entire career, Danny Boyle has resisted repetition and embraced new cinematic challenges at every opportunity. His leap of faith into the great unknown of science fiction may not have been very commercially successful, but that all turned around one year later with a film about the ultimate underdog. *Slumdog Millionaire* was adapted by Simon Beaufoy (writer of *The Full Monty*) from a novel called *Q & A* by Vikas Swarup, and the film was made in the heart of Mumbai. In many ways, filming in the chaotic metropolis of Mumbai provided Boyle with an opportunity to lessen his grip on the details and for the vivacity he constantly seeks to flood the project automatically. When most films are made in such specific and prescribed circumstances, the variables are usually painstakingly eliminated, but in Mumbai, as Boyle explains, it's all but impossible. "It isn't a controlled environment . . . It does make you rethink the way you work straight away. If you want to control Mumbai or change it, or alter it, you might as well go home, because you're just going to waste your money."[37] For all the exotic and unpredictable qualities of the production, the story itself is admittedly more familiar. A number of writers have pointed to the similarities between *Slumdog Millionaire* and the writings of Charles Dickens but, as we've seen in Boyle's other films, there is always room for creativity, personality alongside unabashed homage. To Catherine Bray, he offers a confession for the obvious ties to Dickens: "It's classic storytelling, isn't it? You can't avoid the shadow of Dickens. It's absolute fable. Highs and lows, slight hysteria, convenience, coincidence, good brother, bad brother, impossibly beautiful and unattainable girl taken away whenever you get close."[38] Boyle also explains that India, as opposed to the West, is an appropriate location to set the film because it resembles more the London Dickens wrote about. "[In Mumbai] you still get this sense that Dickens had of this incredible city emerging, burgeoning itself forward, changing every day."[39]

Even with good intentions and an honest attempt to do these characters justice, questions and criticisms arose over Boyle's representation of lower-class India. Some critics in India read the movie not as an inspirational underdog story but an exploitative and stereotypical parable concocted by outsiders.[40] Controversy surrounded the lives of two child actors who played younger versions of the main characters in the film when questions about their compensation were raised. As Boyle explains, there was no ill will meant by calling the main characters "slumdogs," as it is simply a play on the term "underdog." There was also small protest over co-director Loveleen Tandan not being recognized alongside Boyle when he won the Best Director Oscar, but not only has Boyle been upfront and complimentary about her contributions to the film, Tandan herself requested to be ignored from such accolades.[41]

Despite the negative attention, the film went on to become a major success. After winning a Golden Globe and a BAFTA for Best Director, Boyle visited his hometown of Radcliffe, England, to show off his trophies at a local social club. He made a promise to return again if he won the Oscar and, sure enough, he found himself back at St. Mary's Catholic Social Club once again after his big night in Hollywood. Joined by his friends and relatives, including his father and sister, Boyle passed the golden statue around, told stories of his adventures, and drank lemonade. Even after spending more than two decades in the highly competitive television and film industry, Boyle still won't allow the attention to spoil him. "The first thing anybody said to me when I came here with the Golden Globe and the BAFTA was, 'How the bloody hell did anyone like you win a BAFTA?' That's exactly the sort of thing you need saying."[42] At the time of this writing, Boyle's next project appears to be *127 Hours*, a true story about a lone rock climber who survived five days alone after being pinned underneath a boulder.

Consistent with the standards set by the University Press of Mississippi and the "Interviews" series, all interviews within are unabridged and unedited from their original source. Three interviews have been taken from podcasts or video interviews and have been transcribed to the best of my ability.

I would like to thank the following individuals who made this process so enjoyable for me. First, and foremost, I am deeply indebted to Leila Salisbury and Valerie Jones at the University Press of Mississippi for their belief in my ability to do this project justice and for their unending patience and support. Naturally, I cannot express enough gratitude to the authors who were so supportive and allowed me to use their work: Catherine Bray at Film4.com, Tom Charity at the Vancity Theatre, Peter Hawley at Flashpoint Academy, Ambrose Heron at FILMdetail.com, Keith Hopper, Michael Kyrioglou from the DC Film Society, Monika Maurer at the *Richmond Review*, Jeffrey Overstreet at LookingCloser.org, Kevin Polowy at AOL/Moviefone, Hank Sartin at *Time Out Chicago*, Rupert Smith, and Amber Wilkinson at EyeForFilm. Also, there are those publication representatives that were instrumental in the process: Melds Barbara at *TIME Asia*, Joanna Chaundy at the *Independent*, Dan Higgins at PureMovies.com, Claire Hojem and Nick Bland at *Time Out London*, Nicole Holland at *Independent Film Quarterly*, Declan Gibbons at the Galway Film Centre, Matt McAllister at Total Sci-Fi Online, Ian Savage at the *Bury Times*, Brittany Stange at Salon. com, and Rob Winter and Brenda Fernandes at *Sight and Sound*. A special thanks goes to Edwin Page, author of *Ordinary Heroes: The Films of Danny Boyle*, for his guidance and encouragement, Sarah Currant at the BFI National Library for her tremendous support, and to Robert Koontz for his administrative and proofreading assistance.

BD

Notes

1. "Director Danny Returns Home to a Rip-Roaring Welcome," *Bury Times*, March 5, 2009, http://www.burytimes.co.uk/archive/2009/03/05/Bury+News+%28bury_news%29/4168649.Director_Danny_returns_home_to_a_rip_roaring_welcome/.

2. Brian Libby, "Zombies, Smack Addicts, and Starbucks," Salon.com, March 2, 2005, http://dir.salon.com/story/ent/feature/2005/03/02/danny_boyle/index.html.

3. Ibid.

4. Edwin Page, *Ordinary Heroes: The Films of Danny Boyle* (London: Empiricus Books, 2009).

5. Monika Maurer, "Trainspotters," *Richmond Review*, http://www.richmondreview.co.uk/features/maurer01.html.

6. "Director Danny Returns Home."

7. Simon Hattenstone, "Sink or Swim," *The Guardian*, January 28, 2000, http://www.guardian.co.uk/film/2000/jan/28/1.

8. Danny Boyle, "Authors in the Front Line: Danny Boyle in Uzbekistan," *The Sunday Times*, November 28, 2004, http://www.timesonline.co.uk/tol/travel/destinations/asia/article392042.ece.

9. Danny Boyle, "Why the Congo Needs Art As Well As Food," *The Times Online*, November 11, 2008, http://www.timesonline.co.uk/tol/comment/columnists/guest_contributors/article5126664.ece.

10. Ibid.

11. Ronan Bennett, "Lean, Mean, and Cruel," *Sight and Sound* 5, no. 1 (1995): 34–37.

12. Keith Hopper, "*Trainspotting*: The Choice of a New Generation," *Film West*, no. 24 (Spring 1996), http://www.iol.ie/~galfilm/filmwest/24train.htm.

13. Kenneth Turan, "*Trainspotting*: Talkin' 'bout Their Lost Generation," *Los Angeles Times*, July 19, 1996, http://www.calendarlive.com/movies/reviews/cl-movie 960719 5,0,6595973.story.

14. Peter Travers, "*Trainspotting*," *Rolling Stone*, no. 740 (August 8, 1996), http://www.rollingstone.com/reviews/movie/5947253/review/5947254/trainspotting.

15. Hopper, "*Trainspotting*."

16. Ibid.

17. Libby, "Zombies, Smack Addicts, and Starbucks."

18. Hank Sartin, "Boyle's Orders," *Time Out Chicago*, November 13–19, 2008, http://chicago.timeout.com/articles/film/68829/interview-with-slumdog-millionaire-director-danny-boyle.

19. Stephen Short, "The Leo Factor," *TIME Asia*, February 21, 2000, http://www.time.com/time/asia/magazine/2000/0221/cinema.boyle.html.

20. All figures from Box Office Mojo.com.

21. Tom Charity, "Smack My Beach Up," *Time Out London*, January 26–February 2, 2000.

22. Dennis Lim, "The Space Odyssey of Danny Boyle," *New York Times*, July 8, 2007, http://www.nytimes.com/2007/07/08/movies/08lim.html.

23. Tom Charity, "All the Rage," *Time Out London*, October 30–November 6, 2002.

24. Ibid.

25. Sandy Hunter, "*28 Days Later*: An Interview with Danny Boyle," *RES* magazine, May 21, 2003, http://www.res.com/magazine/articles/28dayslateraninterviewwithdannyboyle_2003-05-21.html.

26. Ibid.

27. Ibid.

28. Ibid.

29. Brendan MacDevette, "Danny Boyle," *Independent Film Quarterly*, 2005, http://www.independentfilmquarterly.com/ifq/interviews/dannyboyle.htm.

30. Jeffrey Overstreet, "Movies with Morals," LookingCloser.org, February 2005, http://lookingcloser.org/2005/03/danny-boyle-the-looking-closer-interview-feb-2005/.

31. Michael Kyrioglou, "Q&A with Danny Boyle, Director of Millions," DC Film Society, March 7, 2005, http://www.dcfilmsociety.org/storyboard0503.htm#millions.

32. Roger Ebert, "Millions," March 18, 2005, http://rogerebert.suntimes.com/apps/pbcs .dll/article?AID=/20050317/REVIEWS/50309002/1023.

33. Amber Wilkinson, "Sunshine Superman," Eye For Film.com, March 2007, http://www .eyeforfilm.co.uk/feature.php?id=346.

34. Kevin Polowy, "2007's Space Odyssey: Q&A with *Sunshine* Director Danny Boyle," AOL/Moviefone, July 2007, http://movies.aol.com/celebrity-interview/danny-boyle-sunshine.

35. Ibid.

36. Wilkinson, "Sunshine Superman."

37. Catherine Bray, "*Slumdog Millionaire*: Danny Boyle Interview," *4Talent* magazine, December 2008, http://catherinebray.wordpress.com/2009/02/03/danny-boyle-slumdog-millionaire/.

38. Ibid.

39. Sartin, "Boyle's Orders."

40. Mark Magnier, "Indians Don't Feel Good about *Slumdog Millionaire*," *LA Times*, January 24, 2009, http://articles.latimes.com/2009/jan/24/world/fg-india-slumdog24.

41. John Jurgensen, "The Co-Pilot of Slumdog," *Wall Street Journal*, February 1, 2009, http://online.wsj.com/article/SB123146019434866263.html?mod=googlenews_wsj.

42. "Director Danny Returns Home."

Chronology

1956   Born on October 20 near Manchester in Radcliffe, England. His father, Frank Boyle, was a laborer born in England to an Irish family and his mother was from Ballinasloe, Ireland.

1968   Attends Thornleigh Salesian College in nearby Bolton.

1970   At fourteen, Danny decides to apply at a seminary near Wigan in order to follow his mother's wishes for him to become a Catholic priest. Before his decision was final, Father Conway, a priest, convinces him that he was not meant for priesthood. Soon after, Danny becomes interested in theatre.

1975   Finishes his schooling at Thornleigh.

1978   Graduates from the University of Bangor in Wales. Soon, he begins working with the Joint Stock Theatre Company.

1982   Becomes artistic director for the Royal Court Theatre Upstairs.

1983   Begins dating casting director, Gail Stevens.

1985   Becomes deputy director of the Royal Court Theatre. His first daughter, Grace, is born.

1987   Begins his career in television as a producer on *The Rockingham Shoot* and gets his first chance as a director with *Scout* and *The Venus de Milo Instead*.

1989   Continues his work for the BBC as producer on Alan Clarke's *Elephant* and director on *Monkeys* and *The Hen House*. He is also both producer and director on *The Nightwatch*.

1990   Directs his first episode of *Inspector Morse* ("Masonic Mysteries"). His son, Gabriel, is born.

1991   Directs his last TV movie until 2001 entitled *For the Greater Good*.

1992   Directs his second episode of *Inspector Morse* ("Cherubim and Seraphim"). His daughter, Caitlin, is born.

1993   Directs three episodes of *Mr. Wroe's Virgins* ("Leah's Story,"

"Joanna's Story," and "Hannah's Story") and one episode of *Screenplay* ("Not Even God Is Wise Enough").

1994   Releases *Shallow Grave*, his feature film directorial debut.

1996   Releases *Trainspotting*, a smash hit in the U.K. and abroad. The film successfully brings rejuvenation and attention to Britain's film industry.

1997   Along with Andrew Macdonald, Boyle is executive producer on *Twin Town*, a Welsh film by Kevin Allen. Releases *A Life Less Ordinary*, his first "Hollywood film" that is seen by many as a failure.

2000   Releases *The Beach*, his second Hollywood production made with the largest budget he has worked with. Despite Leonardo DiCaprio's star power, the film is considered a flop.

2001   Directs two films for BBC television, *Strumpet* and *Vacuuming Completely Nude in Paradise*.

2002   Directs a short film entitled *Alien Love Triangle* that was never released. Directs *28 Days Later . . .* , a sleeper hit whose success helps revive the "zombie film." Boyle separates from his partner of twenty years, Gail Stevens. They live very close so their three children can easily go back and forth, and Stevens has continued to work as casting director for his movies.

2005   Directs *Millions*, a family-friendly film dedicated to his parents.

2007   Directs *Sunshine*, a sci-fi epic with an international cast. The sequel to *28 Days Later . . .* is released (*28 Weeks Later*). Boyle is executive producer as well as an uncredited second unit director.

2008   Releases *Slumdog Millionaire* which was dropped by its distributor, Warner Independent, before Fox Searchlight assumed distribution. The film goes on to be nominated for four Golden Globes, eleven BAFTAs, and ten Academy Awards.

2009   On February 22, *Slumdog Millionaire* wins big at the Oscars, taking home prizes including Best Screenplay, Best Picture, and Best Director for Danny. Announces his next project entitled *127 Hours*, a true story about hiker Aron Ralston who spent five days pinned under a rock until he amputated his own arm and survived.

2010   Announces that he will return to working in theatre with a production of *Frankenstein* for the U.K. National Theatre.

Filmography

Short Films

2002
ALIEN LOVE TRIANGLE
Production Company: Figment Films
Producer: Andrew Macdonald
Line Producer: Betsy Danbury
Director: **Danny Boyle**
Screenplay: John Hodge
Cinematography: Brian Tufano
Production Design: Andrew McAlpine
Set Decoration: Anna Pinnock
Editing: Tariq Anwar
Music: Simon Boswell
Cast: Kenneth Branagh (Steven Chesterman), Alice Connor (Sarah), Courteney Cox (Alice), Heather Graham (Elizabeth)
Color, 30 minutes

Feature Films

1994
SHALLOW GRAVE
Production Company: Channel Four Films, Figment Films in association with The Glasgow Film Fund
Producer: Andrew Macdonald
Executive Producer: Allan Scott
Director: **Danny Boyle**
Screenplay: John Hodge
Cinematography: Brian Tufano

Production Design: Kave Quinn
Art Direction: Zoe MacLeod
Editing: Masahiro Hirakubo
Music: Simon Boswell
Cast: Kerry Fox (Juliet Miller), Christopher Eccleston (David Stephens), Ewan McGregor (Alex Law), Ken Stott (Detective Inspector McCall), Keith Allen (Hugo), Colin McCredie (Cameron)
35mm, Widescreen (1.85:1), Color, 92 minutes

1996
TRAINSPOTTING
Production Company: Channel Four Films, Figment Films, The Noel Gay Motion Picture Company
Producer: Andrew Macdonald
Co-Producer: Christopher Figg (uncredited)
Director: **Danny Boyle**
Screenplay: John Hodge, based on a novel by Irvine Welsh
Cinematography: Brian Tufano
Production Design: Kave Quinn
Art Direction: Tracey Gallacher
Editing: Masahiro Hirakubo
Cast: Ewan McGregor (Renton), Ewen Bremner (Spud), Jonny Lee Miller (Sick Boy), Kevin McKidd (Tommy), Robert Carlyle (Begbie), Kelly Macdonald (Diane), Peter Mullan (Swanney), James Cosmo (Mr. Renton), Eileen Nicholas (Mrs. Renton), Susan Vidler (Allison), Pauline Lynch (Lizzy), Shirley Henderson (Gail), Stuart McQuarrie (Gavin/US Tourist), Irvine Welsh (Mikey Forrester)
35mm, Widescreen (1.78:1), Color, 94 minutes

1997
TWIN TOWN
Production Company: Agenda, Aimimage Productions, Figment Films, Polygram Filmed Entertainment
Producer: Peter McAleese
Executive Producer: **Danny Boyle**, Andrew Macdonald
Director: Kevin Allen
Screenplay: Kevin Allen, Paul Durden
Cinematography: John Mathieson
Production Design: Pat Campbell

Art Direction: Dave Arrowsmith, Jean Kerr
Editing: Oral Norrie Ottey
Music: Mark Thomas
Cast: Llyr Ifans (Julian Lewis), Rhys Ifans (Jeremy Lewis), Dorien Thomas (Greyo), Dougray Scott (Terry Walsh), Buddug Williams (Mrs. Mort), Ronnie Williams (Mr. Mort), Huw Ceredig (Fatty Lewis), Rachel Scorgie (Adie Lewis), Di Botcher (Jean Lewis), Mary Allen (Olive), Paul Durden (Taxi Driver), David Hayman (Dodgy), Kevin Allen (TV Presenter)
35mm, Widescreen (1.85:1), Color, 99 minutes

A LIFE LESS ORDINARY
Production Company: Channel Four Films, Figment Films, Polygram Filmed Entertainment
Producer: Andrew Macdonald
Line Producer: Margaret Hilliard
Animation Producer: Sophie Byrne
Director: **Danny Boyle**
Screenplay: John Hodge
Cinematography: Brian Tufano
Production Design: Kave Quinn
Art Direction: Tracey Gallacher
Editing: Masahiro Hirakubo
Music: David Arnold
Cast: Ewan McGregor (Robert Lewis), Cameron Diaz (Celine Naville), Holly Hunter (O'Reilly), Delroy Lindo (Jackson), Dan Hedaya (Gabriel), Ian McNeice (Mayhew), Frank Kanig (Ted), Mel Winkler (Francis "Frank" Naville), Stanley Tucci (Elliot Zweikel), Anne Cullimore Decker (Violet Eldred Gesteten), K. K. Dodds (Lily), Tony Shalhoub (Al), Christopher Gorham (Walt), Ian Holm (Naville), Maury Chaykin (Tod Johnson), Timothy Olyphant (Hiker)
35mm, Anamorphic Widescreen (2.35:1), Color, 103 minutes

2000
THE BEACH
Production Company: Figment Films
Producer: Andrew Macdonald
Co-Producer: Callum McDougall
Director: **Danny Boyle**
Screenplay: John Hodge, based on a novel by Alex Garland

Cinematography: Darius Khondji
Production Design: Andrew McAlpine
Art Direction: Ricky Eyres, Suchartanun "Kai" Kuladee, Rod McLean, Ben Scott
Editing: Masahiro Hirakubo
Music: Angelo Badalamenti
Cast: Leonardo DiCaprio (Richard), Daniel York (Hustler), Patcharawan Patarakijjanon (Hotel Receptionist), Virginie Ledoyen (Françoise), Guillaume Canet (Étienne), Robert Carlyle (Daffy), Peter Youngblood Hills (Zeph), Jerry Swindall (Sammy), Paterson Joseph (Keaty), Zelda Tinska (Sonja), Victoria Smurfit (Weathergirl), Daniel Caltagirone (Unhygenix), Peter Gevisser (Gregorio), Lars Arentz-Hansen (Bugs), Tilda Swinton (Sal), Lidija Zovkic (Mirjana), Samuel Gough (Guitarman), Staffan Kihlbom (Christo), Jukka Hiltunen (Karl), Magnus Lindgren (Sten)
35mm anamorphic, Anamorphic Widescreen (2.35:1), Color, 119 minutes
Language: English, French, Swedish, Thai, Serbo-Croatian

2002
28 DAYS LATER . . .
Production Company: DNA Films, British Film Council (UK Film Council)
Producer: Andrew Macdonald
Line Producer: Robert How
Director: **Danny Boyle**
Screenplay: Alex Garland
Cinematography: Anthony Dod Mantle
Production Design: Mark Tildesley
Art Direction: Mark Digby, Rod Gorwood, Patrick Rolfe
Editing: Chris Gill
Music: John Murphy
Cast: Cillian Murphy (Jim), Naomie Harris (Selena), Noah Huntley (Mark), Christopher Dunne (Jim's Father), Emma Hitching (Jim's Mother), Alexander Delamere (Mr. Bridges), Kim McGarrity (Mr. Bridges' Daughter), Brendan Gleeson (Frank), Megan Burns (Hannah), Luke Mably (Private Clifton), Stuart McQuarrie (Sergeant Farrell), Ricci Harnett (Corporal Mitchell), Leo Bill (Private Jones), Junior Laniyan (Private Bell), Ray Panthaki (Private Bedford), Christopher Eccleston (Major Henry West)
Video (PAL)/8mm/35mm, Widescreen (1.85:1), Color, 113 minutes

2004
MILLIONS
Production Company: Pathé Pictures International (presents), UK Film Council (in association with), BBC Films (in association with), Mission Pictures, Inside Track 2 (produced in association with), Ingenious Film Partners
Producer: Graham Broadbent, Andrew Hauptman, Damian Jones
Executive Producer: François Ivernal, Cameron McCracken, Duncan Reid, David M. Thompson
Associate Producer: Katie Goodson
Co-Producer: Tracey Seaward
Director: **Danny Boyle**
Screenplay: Frank Cottrell Boyce
Cinematography: Anthony Dod Mantle
Production Design: Mark Tildesley
Art Direction: Denis Schnegg
Editing: Chris Gill
Music: John Murphy
Cast: Alex Etel (Damian), Lewis McGibbon (Anthony), James Nesbitt (Ronnie), Daisy Donovan (Dorothy), Christopher Fulford (The Man), Pearce Quigley (Community Policeman), Jane Hogarth (Mum), Alun Armstrong (St. Peter), Enzo Cilenti (St. Francis), Nasser Memarzia (St. Joseph), Kathryn Pogson (St. Clare), Harry Kirkham (St. Nicholas), Cornelius Macarthy (Gonzaga), Kolade Agboke (Ambrosio), Leslie Phillips (Leslie Phillips), James Quinn (Estate Agent), Mark Chatterton (Headteacher), Toby Walton (Damian's Teacher), Frank Cottrell Boyce (Nativity Teacher), Gunnar Winbergh (Eli), Christian Rubeck (Jerome), Guy Flanagan (All Saint 3), Philippa Howarth (Tricia), Billy Hyland (Keegan), John Nugent (Graham), Steve Garti (Terry), Alice Grice (Maria), Dale Stringer (Fairclough)
35mm, Widescreen (1.85:1), Color, 98 minutes

2007
SUNSHINE
Production Company: DNA Films, Ingenious Film Partners, Moving Picture Company (MPC), UK Film Council
Producer: Andrew Macdonald
Co-Producer: Bernard Bellew
Director: **Danny Boyle**
Screenplay: Alex Garland

Cinematography: Alwin H. Kuchler
Production Design: Mark Tildesley
Art Direction: Gary Freeman, Stephen Morahan, Denis Schnegg, David Warren
Editing: Chris Gill
Music: John Murphy
Cast: Cliff Curtis (Searle), Chipo Chung (Icarus) (voice), Cillian Murphy (Capa), Michelle Yeoh (Corazon), Hiroyuki Sanada (Kaneda), Rose Byrne (Cassie), Benedict Wong (Trey), Chris Evans (Mace), Troy Garity (Harvey), Mark Strong (Pinbacker), Paloma Baeza (Capa's Sister), Archie Macdonald (Child), Sylvie Macdonald (Child)
35mm/65mm, Anamorphic Widescreen (2.35:1), Color, 107 minutes

28 WEEKS LATER
Production Company: Fox Atomic, DNA Films, UK Film Council, Figment Films, Sociedad General de Cine (SOGECINE) S.A., Koan Films
Producer: Enrique López Lavigne, Andrew Macdonald, Allon Reich
Executive Producer: **Danny Boyle**, Alex Garland
Co-Producer: Bernard Bellew
Director: Juan Carlos Fresnadillo
Additional Second Unit Director: **Danny Boyle** (uncredited)
Screenplay: Rowan Joffe, Juan Carlos Fresnadillo, Enrique López Lavigne, Jesús Olmo
Cinematography: Enrique Chediak
Production Design: Mark Tildesley
Art Direction: Patrick Rolfe, Denis Schnegg
Editing: Chris Gill
Music: John Murphy
Cast: Robert Carlyle (Don), Catherine McCormack (Alice), Rose Byrne (Scarlet), Jeremy Renner (Doyle), Harold Perrineau (Flynn), Idris Elba (Stone), Imogen Poots (Tammy), Mackintosh Muggleton (Andy), Amanda Walker (Sally), Shahid Ahmed (Jacob), Garfield Morgan (Geoff), Emily Beecham (Karen)
16mm/35mm/Video (DV), Widescreen (1.85:1), Color, 99 minutes

2008
SLUMDOG MILLIONAIRE
Production Company: Celador Films (presents), Film4 (presents), Pathé Pictures International

Producer: Christian Colson
Executive Producer: Tessa Ross, Paul Smith
Co-Executive Producer: François Ivernal, Cameron McCracken
Associate Producer: Ivana Mackinnon
Co-Producer: Paul Ritchie
Line Producer: Tabrez Noorani
Director: **Danny Boyle**
Co-Director: Loveleen Tandan
Screenplay: Simon Beaufoy, based on the novel *Q & A* by Vikas Swarup
Cinematography: Anthony Dod Mantle
Production Design: Mark Digby
Art Direction: Abhishek Redkar
Editing: Chris Dickens
Music: A. R. Rahman
Cast: Dev Patel (Jamal K. Malik), Saurabh Shukla (Sergeant Srinivas), Anil Kapoor (Prem), Rajendranath Zutshi (Director), Jeneva Talwar (Vision Mixer), Frieda Pinto (Latika), Irrfan Khan (Police Inspector), Azharuddin Mohammed Ismail (Youngest Salim), Ayush Mahesh Khedekar (Youngest Jamal), Jira Banjara (Airport Security Guard), Sheikh Wali (Airport Security Guard), Mahesh Manjrekar (Javed), Sanchita Choudhary (Jamal's Mother), Himanshu Tyagi (Mr. Nanda), Sharib Hashmi (Prakash), Virendra Chatterjee (Slum Man), Feroze Khan (Amitabh Bachchan), Sunil Kumar Agrawal (Mr. Chi), Virender Kumar (Man on Fire), Devesh Rawal (Blue Boy), Rubina Ali (Youngest Latika), Ankur Vikal (Maman), Tiger (Punnoose), Chirag Parmar (Young Arvind), Farzana Ansari (Latika's Friend), Tanay Chheda (Middle Jamal), Ashutosh Lobo Gajiwala (Middle Salim), Siddesh Patil (Older Arvind), Tanvi Ganesh Lonkar (Middle Latika), Madhur Mittal (Older Salim)
35mm/Digital/Video (HDTV), Anamorphic Widescreen (2.35:1), Color, 120 minutes
Language: English, Hindi

Television

1987
THE ROCKINGHAM SHOOT
Production Company: BBC Northern Ireland
Producer: **Danny Boyle**

Director: Kieran Hickey
Screenplay: John McGahem
Cinematography: Philip Dawson
Cast: Bosco Hogan (Reilly), Niall Toibin (Canon), Marie Kean (Mrs. Reilly), Tony Rohr (Magician), Oliver Maguire (Sergeant), Ian McElhinney (John Reilly), Hilary Reynolds (Mary Armstrong), John Olohan (Garda Mullins), Gerard McSorley (Garda Casey), Libby Smyth (First Teacher), Carmel McDonnell (Second Teacher), Ronan Wilmot (Molloy), Dick Holland (White), William Walker (Collins), John Keyes (Gamekeeper), Tony Coleman (Dublin Detective 1), Michael Gormley (Dublin Detective 2)

SCOUT
Production Company: BBC Northern Ireland
Producer: **Danny Boyle**
Director: **Danny Boyle**
Screenplay: Frank McGuinness
Cast: Ray McAnally (Palmer), Stephen Rea (Marshall), Colin Connor (Cherry), Michael Liebman (Dodd), Gerard O'Hare (Turkington), Lloyd Hutchinson (Shields), Jeremy Chapman (Keevney), Paul Ryder (O'Toole)

THE VENUS DE MILO INSTEAD
Production Company: British Broadcasting Corporation (BBC)
Director: **Danny Boyle**
Screenplay: Anne Devlin
Cast: Brigid Erin Bates (Mrs. Hogg), Lorcan Cranitch (Mr. Scott), Jeananne Crowley (Mrs. Grey), Iain Cuthbertson (Headmaster), Jean-Claude Deret (French Proprietor), Tony Doyle (Courier), Sylvie Favre (French Proprietor's Wife), Ann Hasson (Miss Black), B. J. Hogg (Painter), Trudy Kelly (Mrs. McIllvaine), Aine McCartney (Mrs. McMullen), Ruth McGuigan (Tracey), Mark Mulholland (Policeman), Leila Webster (Mrs. Parks), Brenda Winter (Mrs. Wishart)
60 minutes

1989
ELEPHANT
Production Company: BBC Northern Ireland
Producer: **Danny Boyle**

Director: Alan Clarke
Screenplay: Bernard MacLaverty
Cinematography: Philip Dawson, John Ward
Editing: Don O'Donovan
Cast: Gary Walker, Bill Hamilton, Michael Foyle, Danny Small, Robert J. Taylor, Joe Cauley, Joe McGee, Patrick Condren, Andrew Downs, Terry Doyle, Michael Liebman, Gavin Bloomer, Barry Brent, Paul Nemeer, Sam Doyle, Burt Murray, Tim Loane, Kenny Harris, Paddy Rocks, Ken McIlroy, Hamish Fyfe, Trevor Moore, William Walker, Brian Giffen, Billy Dee, Michael Fieldhouse, William McAllister, Alan Craig, Stephen Potter, David McDade, Mark O'Donnell
16mm, Color, 38 minutes

THE NIGHTWATCH
Production Company: BBC Northern Ireland
Producer: **Danny Boyle**
Director: **Danny Boyle**
Screenplay: Ray Brennan
Cinematography: Philip Dawson
Editing: Roger Ford-Hutchinson
Cast: James Cosmo (James Smithson), Tony Doyle (John Healey), Michael Feast (Phillip Howard), Don Fellows (Paul Arland), Leslie Grantham (David Smallman), Inge Ipenburg (Prostitute), Zeff Van Heligan (Joop Doderer)
Color, 50 minutes

MONKEYS
Director: **Danny Boyle**
Cast: Manning Redwood (John DeLorean), William Hootkins (James Hoffman), Harry Ditson (Benedict J. Tisa), Clarke Peters (William Morgan Hetrick), Bob Sherman (John Vincenza/Valestra), Martha Thimmesch (John DeLorean's Assistant)

THE HEN HOUSE
Production Company: BBC Northern Ireland
Producer: Robert Cooper
Director: **Danny Boyle**
Screenplay: Frank McGuinness
Editing: Roy Sharman

Cast: Sinéad Cusack (Lily), Tony Doyle (McCloskey)
60 minutes

1990
INSPECTOR MORSE (episode: "Masonic Mysteries")
Production Company: Zenith Entertainment, Central Independent Television
Producer: David Lascelles
Executive Producer: Ted Childs
Associate Producer: John Davis
Director: **Danny Boyle**
Screenplay: Colin Dexter (characters), Julian Mitchell (written by)
Cinematography: Paul Wheeler
Production Design: Terry Ackland-Snow
Art Direction: Stephen Scott
Editing: Robert C. Dearberg
Music: Barrington Pheloung
Cast: John Thaw (Chief Inspector Morse), Kevin Whately (Detective Sergeant Lewis), Madelaine Newton (Beryl Newsome), Ian McDiarmid (Hugo De Vries), Celestine Randall (Sandra Machin), Roland Oliver (Conductor), John Arthur (Hall Porter), James Grout (Chief Superintendent Strange), Richard Kane (Chief Inspector Bottomley), Steven Elliot (Officious Constable), Richard Huw (Detective Constable Dearden), Iain Cuthbertson (Desmond McNutt), Mark Strong (PC Mike Butterworth)

1991
FOR THE GREATER GOOD
Production Company: British Broadcasting Corporation (BBC)
Director: **Danny Boyle**
Screenplay: G. F. Newman
Cinematography: Nigel Walters
Editing: Clare Douglas
Cast: John Arthur (Prison Officers' Spokesman), Eileen Benskin (Prison Psychologist), Connie Booth (Naomi Balliol), Chas Bryer (P.O. Suckley), Peter Cellier (Clive Hough MP), Jonathan Cullen (George Roeves), Michael Culver (Sir Christopher St. Place), Roy Dotrice (Charles Truman MP), Julian Fellowes (Neville Marsham), David Harewood (David West), Brian Hayes (Himself), David Henry (Chief Whip), Bernard Horsfall (Prime Minister)
150 minutes (3 episodes)

1992
INSPECTOR MORSE (episode: "Cherubim & Seraphim")
Production Company: Zenith Entertainment, Central Independent Television
Producer: Deirdre Keir
Executive Producer: Ted Childs
Director: **Danny Boyle**
Screenplay: Colin Dexter (characters), Julian Mitchell (written by)
Cinematography: Peter Greenhalgh
Production Design: Maurice Cain
Editing: Kevin Lester
Music: Barrington Pheloung
Cast: John Thaw (Chief Inspector Morse), Kevin Whately (Detective Sergeant Lewis), Liza Walker (Vicky Wilson), Jason Isaacs (Dr. Desmond Collier), Charlotte Chatton (Marilyn Garrett), Charlie Caine (Charlie Paget), Anna Chancellor (Sally Smith), Freddie Brooks (Jacko Lever), Sorcha Cusack (Joyce Garrett), Edwina Day (Gwen Morse), Celia Blaker (Nurse), Matt Terdre (Ken Lewis), Glen Mead (Wayne Garrett), Phillip Joseph (Keith Garrett), Isla Blair (Janey Wilson), Christopher Benjamin (Professor Furlong), James Grout (Chief Superintendent Strange), John Junkin (Chief Inspector Holroyd)

1993
MR. WROE'S VIRGINS (episodes: "Leah's Story," "Joanna's Story," "Hannah's Story," and "Martha's Story")
Production Company: British Broadcasting Corporation (BBC)
Producer: John Chapman
Executive Producer: Michael Wearing
Associate Producer: Rosalind Wolfes
Director: **Danny Boyle**
Screenplay: Jane Rogers
Cinematography: Brian Tufano
Production Design: John Coleman, Catherine Kelly, Ruth Kelly, Jane Rogers
Editor: Masahiro Hirakubo
Music: Brian Eno, Roger Eno
Cast: Jonathan Pryce (John Wroe), Kathy Burke (Martha), Minnie Driver (Leah), Kerry Fox (Hannah), Freddie Jones (Tobias), Catherine Kelly (Rachel), Ruth Kelly (Rebekah), Moya Brady (Dinah), Lia Williams (Joanna), Nicholas Woodeson (Brother Moses), Stefan Escreet (Samuel

Walker), Fine Time Fontayne (Brother Paine), Tony Haygarth (Hannah's Father), Michelle Holmes (Annie), Chris Brailsford (Leah's Father), Danny Davies (Caleb), Mark Southworth (Leah's Soldier)
35mm, 1.33:1, Color, 240 minutes (4 episodes)

SCREENPLAY (episode: "Not Even God Is Wise Enough")
Production Company: British Broadcasting Corporation (BBC)
Producer: Colin Ludlow
Director: **Danny Boyle**
Screenplay: Biyi Bandele-Thomas
Cast: Colin Farrell

2001
STRUMPET
Production Company: British Broadcasting Corporation (BBC), Destiny Films
Producer: Martin Carr
Director: **Danny Boyle**
Screenplay: Jim Cartwright
Cinematography: Anthony Dod Mantle
Editor: Chris Gill
Music: John Murphy
Cast: Josh Cole (Record Engineer), David Crellin (Curdy), Stephen Da Costa (Perry), Christopher Eccleston (Strayman), Amanda Fairclough (Strumpet's Mother), Genna G (Strumpet), Graeme Hawley (Producer), Jonathan Ryland (Colonel Parker), Stephen Walters (Knockoff), Bernard Wrigley, Adam Zane (Tim)
Digital Video (DV), Color, 72 minutes

VACUUMING COMPLETELY NUDE IN PARADISE
Production Company: British Broadcasting Corporation (BBC), Destiny Films
Producer: Martin Carr
Executive Producer: Hilary Salmon, David M. Thompson
Associate Producer: Des Hughes
Director: **Danny Boyle**
Screenplay: Jim Cartwright
Cinematography: Anthony Dod Mantle
Production Design: John Coleman

Art Direction: Emer O'Sullivan, Sue Pow
Editor: Chris Gill
Music: John Murphy
Cast: Timothy Spall (Tommy Rag), Michael Begley (Pete), Katy Cavanagh (Sheila), Caroline Ashley (Uki), Alice Barry (Lorna), Terry Barry (Ted), Julie Brown (Receptionist), James Cartwright (De Kid), Lorraine Cheshire (Hot Pot), Keith Clifford (Sidney), David Crellin (Mr. Ron), James Foster (Porter), Sandra Gough (Spaniard), Renny Krupinski (Pockmark), Rodney Litchfield (Throat), Caroline Pegg (Boney Lyn), Maggie Tagney (Stonecheeks), Miriam Watkins (Claywoman)
Digital Video (DV), Color, 76 minutes

Music Video

1996
LUST FOR LIFE
Production Company: Palomar Pictures International
Director: **Danny Boyle**
Cinematography: Brian Tufano
Editor: John Mallerman, David Booth
Artist: Iggy Pop

Danny Boyle: Interviews

Lean, Mean, and Cruel

Ronan Bennett/1995

From *Sight and Sound* 5, no. 1 (1995). Copyright British Film Institute. Reprinted with permission.

Danny Boyle doesn't like talking about "ideas" in his new film, *Shallow Grave*. He doesn't like talking about ideas in film in general because, he says, it's pompous, self-conscious, and patronizing to the audience. It's an interesting position, coming from a man whose early career as a director was in theatre, first with the radical Joint Stock Company, then with the Royal Court—the playwrights he has worked with include Edward Bond and Howard Barker. Most recently, Boyle has been working in television, in shows as various as *Inspector Morse* and the serial *Mr. Wroe's Virgins*.

As a writer, I'm the opposite to this. I tend to start, whether it's a novel or a screenplay, with the idea I want to explore rather than the plot. In *A Man You Don't Meet Every Day* (directed by Angela Pope and screened on Channel 4 in November 1994), I wanted to look at the notion of Ireland-meets-England through the encounter between a working-class Irishman, Jim, and a middle-class Englishwoman, Charlotte. With *Love Lies Bleeding* (shown on BBC2 in September 1993), I was trying to tackle political violence in Ireland and suggest that, rather than being the mindless orgy of self-destruction commonly portrayed, it had specific goals: to bring the British government to the negotiating table.

Starting out with such ideas does not mean you finish with them. Deficiencies in talent and technique can take their toll. In the writing itself, things change: what appeared possible or interesting at the beginning may seem, after the first few scenes, ludicrous or redundant. The demands of narrative impose other limitations: I have always been aware of the need to keep an audience with you as you try to plant the idea of the piece, and I have never been shy of using thrills and spills to achieve this. Ideas in film are, I believe, much more fragile, more vulnerable to eclipse, than those in novels or theatre. Given the economy of film, it is never possible to answer questions, only to raise them. If you're not careful, the thrills can obscure the point you're trying to make; the spills can swamp the idea (a criticism I would make of my own work).

There are obvious dangers in talking this way about one's work, as Boyle points out. You can find yourself making claims about what you've done which are simply not true; you can end up believing your own propaganda. In the search to dignify your work with some kind of intellectual respectability, you can easily start to feel superior about the "lowlier" aspirations of film-making—such as entertaining the audience.

It is primarily as entertainment that Boyle wants *Shallow Grave* to be seen. It is a low-budget British film—exciting, fast, witty, and, in a most unBritish way, unabashed about exhibiting style. It comes over as confident and deliberately provocative. The direction is energetic, moving the narrative along with speed and economy. The design, particularly the use of strong colors, lends the film a cartoonish feel heightened both by the burlesque violence—intended, as in cartoons, to be comic rather than shocking—and by the improbable behavior of the main characters.

The story concerns three affluent late twenty-somethings (played by Kerry Fox, Christopher Eccleston, and Ewan McGregor) living in a smart New Town flat in Edinburgh, who take in a lodger (Keith Allen) who soon afterwards dies in his bedroom of a drug overdose. The trio discover a suitcase full of money among the dead man's belongings. They decide to keep it and dispose of the body secretly. Then their troubles begin. As with *Blood Simple* and *The Treasure of the Sierra Madre*, the audience watches illicit riches corrode the bonds of friendship and morality holding the three together.

For me, the film never escapes predictability, though Boyle says audiences so far have not guessed the ending. But the real problem I found was the freezing and cruel emptiness at the film's heart. The absence of any character to sympathize or engage with made it hard to find an emotional response as the unpleasant, greedy trio destroyed themselves and each other.

Such opinions bounce off Boyle, who seems to be saying that he has turned his back on the kind of "pompous" film and drama he used to make in favor of movies for the Bart Simpson generation. He takes criticism well. There is no trace of defensiveness. But he emphatically rejects my argument that the film lacks ideas: "You're a snob, an absolute snob."

Ronan Bennett: How did it all start?

Danny Boyle: The script was written by John Hodge, a doctor, and worked on by Hodge and Andrew MacDonald, the film's eventual producer. At some point it found its way to David Action at Channel 4, who said he was interested, so they started to look for a director. They sent the script out to about twenty directors altogether, which is very much Andrew's way. A lot of people turned it down, a lot thought it was cruel and heartless. When I read it I thought it was a really exciting British script—clean and mean and truly cinematic in the way the Billy Wilder films are. I thought, I've got to do this. When I went for the audition I said it reminded me of *Blood Simple*, in its commitment to narrative and plot, which got me off on the right foot. Then we went into Channel 4 and began to work on the script together, and I said what I would try to do, and the kind of people we would cast. It was the fast track. Channel 4 said, "If you can get the Glasgow Film Fund to give you £150,000 we'll give you £850,000. Can you make it for that amount?" We said yes, and started to work out how we could make it for £1 million.

RB: Did that mean you had to change things, drop things?

DB: Not at all, because John was very clear-minded about how to get a film made, and he'd written it so it could be made for virtually nothing, which is why 80 percent of the script takes place inside the flat. He had used as few locations as possible, and those locations he had included were simple ones. The feel of the flat was a big artistic decision in the way we presented the film. We took the risk that we would try to make the film cinematic through our use of interior space rather than what is traditional, which is exterior space. So we built a frighteningly enormous set in a warehouse in Glasgow and spent the vast proportion of our budget on that element. We could have done the film like an early Polanski, using the interior as an oppressive, claustrophobic space, in a way we're fairly used to in Britain. But one of the unusual things about Edinburgh is these New Town flats—a small door leading to a universe of space. I wanted the audience to look at this big and sexy space and think, I'd like to live in that. And we opted for evocative colors rather than the neutralizing, pastel shades we all tend to live in.

RB: You often hear writers talking about how they produce a beautiful script and then other people—the director, the producer, the script editor—get their hands on it and it goes from a work of art to something much less. My own experience of screenwriting has so far been restricted to British television and film producers—I don't know what it's like in the U.S.—but I wouldn't hesitate to acknowledge that despite frequent points of disagreement and high tension, my scripts have benefited from that kind of collaboration. How did that process work for *Shallow Grave*?

DB: It worked very well. We all agreed that we would like the plot to be more complex, which is something Channel 4 was pushing for as well. They were exemplary in the way they dealt with it—they kept hitting us with good strong suggestions, but we were free to use them or not. To my mind, the script knew exactly where it was going and was heading there at a hundred miles per hour, it was just a question of increasing its trajectory. John writes in a lean, exciting way—he just writes dialogue, but you can see the film immediately when you read it. I've had less than wonderful experiences with writers in the past, for which I take full responsibility. I tend to feel that what you have to do is explain to the writer beforehand what you feel about their script and if you're right, then you should work together. But if you're completely off the mark, you shouldn't be working on the project. I told them how I saw it, they thought it was right, and they gave me the job. Then you can abandon your objectivity and head off on this journey together.

We worked very much as a team—it was always our desire that the three of us, Andrew, John, and I, should be equally creative. So we took the same fee, the same percentage points. I found it very liberating to sacrifice some of the ego and control you expect to have as a director.

RB: Was sorting out the fee and the points important?

DB: Andrew said from the beginning that it would be equal for everybody and everybody else who came into the project at later stages. They were all paid equivalent equals—not actual equals because they all work for different lengths of time, and obviously a cameraman is paid more than a loader, but, on a scale, it was the equivalent.

It was a very low-budget film, and we never expected it to have the kind of success it has had. It was an attempt to make an invigorating and exciting low-budget British film, which meant the narrative became the principal ingredient. The narrative was our god.

RB: The way you describe it implies that characterization was much less important. Clever plot, but what about the people? One of the criticisms of British film is that it comes out of theatre, with the result that there is too much emphasis on dialogue and character. You've reversed that, haven't you?

DB: Not completely. As soon as you get actors on board—the characters—they become mini-gods. Quite rightly, the actor's obsession is with the integrity of their character. So we did a lot of work on the characters once we started rehearsal. Then there's also the thing that once you cast an actor, you lose sight of what you dreamed the part was about when you first read it—you make a decision, an act of faith in an actor and what they're going to bring to the movie, and from that moment on you can't see it in any other way.

RB: I thought the characterization tended to be done in broad strokes. Alex is quickly established as a cocky little shite, Christopher is the neurotic oddball, a bit of a loner, and there's the woman doctor . . . For me the fact that the characters were underdrawn and came across as deeply unpleasant from the first made it hard to engage with.

DB: I disagree. I think there are other levels. I must admit that I've spent a lot of my career building up plausible characters, which intellectuals find rewarding and interesting. But the public doesn't give a fuck. They have a slightly different agenda. Now you can either despise them for their lack of rigor, or you can in some way embrace them and give them, in terms of a British film, some slightly different things, which is what we were trying to do.

I think one of the interesting things about the characters is that they're used in a way that's about the more cruel side of ourselves. They're not looked at with benevolence—that side of them, which was there at some stage in their lives, isn't explored. Of course, they're all longing to be loved but they are unable to admit that to each other and to build on it, so it becomes a relationship of advantage rather than of co-operation and sharing. The writer has chosen to take a particular moment in their lives, a moment of cruelty. At one point, we were going to call the film *Cruel*.

There is fascinating character development going on, but it's not there in a traditional way because the problem with traditional character development is that audiences are not there primarily to watch a character being drawn. What they want is the excitement and the speed of the journey that cinema can provide.

RB: It sounds as though you've decided what the public likes and you're going to give it to them.

DB: I'd agree with that, except that I'd express it slightly differently. I'd say that in the past I've been pompous in the way I've tried to present work to the audience. We're not in a naive society any more, and there's no real thirst for naive filmmaking. The television plays of the sixties are what I call naive. We've moved on from there now, especially since the eighties. You can't keep trying to recreate *Play for Today*. It's patronizing. You can't preach to people any more.

People today are more sophisticated, highly literate, though they're given no credit for it. Through media they have access to a fabulous library of information for which they don't have to study, they don't have to have time to reflect and quietly absorb. So we tried to make a film that was intelligent entertainment, that didn't patronize people, that said if you want an agenda beyond the narrative, then you can look for it in the film—and it's there, an examination of our modern lives and how you might be at a certain age in your life.

RB: How does it fit with other movies about modern life?

DB: I think it's incredibly healthy for the film world that at Cannes, Kieslowski, who is the great master we all bow down in front of, was lined up to get the Palme d'Or and the pedestal he was on was shaken vigorously by this young punk Quentin Tarantino, who for all his faults is making exciting, dynamic cinema that people want to see.

Personally I love *Au revoir les enfants*, but I don't want to go out there and say to the British public, this is my favorite film and I'm going to make copies of it. We have lived through the war, we have lived through the welfare state. You have to try to keep up with the way society is evolving. One of the main points about *Shallow Grave* is that there are no more victims, no one behaves like a victim.

RB: *Shallow Grave* is very different from your last work for television, *Mr. Wroe's Virgins*.

DB: The BBC is wonderful, but one of the problems with television is the nature of your relationship with the audience. It's there and you take it for granted, and you don't even think to challenge. It's entirely different seeing an audience in front of your film. That was one of the bizarre things about screening the film: I was thinking it was going to the exactly the same as television, where you have no relationship with your audience, but of course it's completely different: the audience is there, live, booing or clapping or walking out or doing whatever. They're teaching you things about your work, changing the film in front of you, even though, supposedly, it's fixed and finished.

RB: What you're describing is something that's almost interactive.

DB: I've got young kids, and they look at lots of stuff on television. I watched *The Simpsons* with them, and I watched them watching this picture of a modern family. It's a very sophisticated, ironic image, one I never had as a child. You can't ignore this image, even if you don't agree with it and you may despise Rupert Murdoch. But I recognize that my children are, in a small part of their consciousness, relating to me through the prism of Bart Simpson, relating to his father Homer. Children are different for having watched Bart Simpson. You have to take that on board.

RB: Working for television, your audience is assured. When you move into feature films, do you feel that you have to make a nod in their direction, give them what they want?

DB: When it works, television is great, as good as any cinema, and in one sense there's no difference. But one of the things that is forced on you when you make a feature is a sense of responsibility towards money, and by extension to the audience. Making a feature film is an invigorating shower of change, you're drenched with a different sensibility.

I'm in awe of public taste. I know that if you can present your work well enough, the public can be very flexible in its reception. We're talking about a relatively small number of people, of course, because of the amount of people who go to see movies. But you have to be in sync with them. I'm a big admirer of Ken Loach's work, but I think one of the problems with *Ladybird Ladybird* is that it felt to me like it was describing a society which Loach had already looked at in much of his previous work. It hadn't moved on, and I'm afraid I think we have.

Books are slightly different because in some ways they are like a diary. As a novelist, I can say this in my book, this is what I want to say, and people can take it or leave it. The stuff I do for television is similar in that respect—as long as I have a narrative and structure that can fit within a television play, I'm given the freedom to say what I want to say and I don't have to make concessions. But in feature films, a writer has to be conscious of the responsibility of manipulating the audience.

RB: I disagree. Where do you start to draw the line? What happens when the producer comes to you and says, I really like this script, but if we had a nude scene in here and a murder there, we'd have a better chance of getting the film made? Do you go along with such suggestions?

DB: If he's a wanker then you just walk away from him. You don't do it by opinion poll, obviously. What you do is remember the last audience you were with and how bored they were by a particular attitude. All that goes into your consciousness and you take it into account when making your film.

RB: What about casting? Did you have your wish list?

DB: If you're doing a film that's going to cost £10 million, then you have to provide interesting casting to try to recoup that money in some way. With a budget of only £1 million, you're much freer—your backers are prepared to leave you to it. We talked about the wish list, but this film was always going to be about three people and we didn't want to imbalance it by trying to approach someone like Gary Oldman, when it would become a film in which everyone would he looking at Gary Oldman. We set out deliberately to make it a partnership of three main performers. The partnership's success was recognized in Dinard when the Best Actor award went to the three of them.

The female character was always an outsider, and we decided she didn't have to be Scottish, so we asked Kerry Fox, who is a New Zealander who worked with me on *Mr. Wroe's Virgins*. She's very chameleon, you don't recognize her from one appearance to another, so though she's experienced, she's also unfamiliar. Then we got Ewan McGregor, who had been in Dennis Potter's *Lipstick on Your Collar*. He has charm coming out of his eardrums, and we wanted that charm for Alex. For Christopher we wanted a gentle giant, someone very big so that when he is threatening it's actually physically frightening. We'd seen Christopher Eccleston in *Let Him Have It* and liked him.

RB: When I first started writing screenplays I was horrified by the way actors were brought together. In *A Man You Don't Meet Every Day*, Harriet Walter met her "mother" during the read-through and then didn't see her again until the day they filmed the scene. I've always been surprised at the lack of time for preparation and the absence of much of a collective or collaborative experience. How long did you have for rehearsal?

DB: I've just watched some shorts, British shorts, made with very little time for preparation or shooting, and you can tell that the actors are just doing what they're told, that they haven't had the time to establish confidence in themselves or the people they're working with in order to make their mark on the film.

For *Shallow Grave*, we had a week. It started with two but got cut to one. We decided that instead of rehearsing in a traditional way, the three actors and myself would move into a flat together and live there for the rehearsal week—cook, watch our favorite videos, watch videos we thought were appropriate, play the music we thought was appropriate. It bound the three of them together in a way we wouldn't have achieved through traditional rehearsals with everyone slipping off to their different hotels. And it was a refresher course in what it was like to share a flat with people.

In the end we also cast John in one of the parts—as Mitchell, the copper's sidekick—because one of the problems for a writer involved day-to-day on the set is the feeling of having nothing to do, of being in the way. The crew were all drawn from Glasgow. One of the things about Britain is that our technicians are the best in the world.

RB: Will you stay in Britain or are you tempted to go to America?

DB: The scale of the success of *Four Weddings and a Funeral* made people respect it. That's healthy: a commercial film that works for an audience, something that values an audience and delivers. If you want to make films that return the money, so that somebody else can make a film after you, you have to get a kid and his girlfriend or her boyfriend into the cinema on a Friday night. They're going to give you their £10 and they want to have an interesting evening, they want to be stimulated, excited. The fact that a British film like *Four Weddings* can do that throughout the world is to be celebrated, because it means that a whole range of more difficult, darker, more peculiar films can come along behind it. I think things look quite good here.

RB: Would you describe yourself as a business-conscious director?

DB: Certainly. I don't think there's anything irresponsible or ugly or callous about that. I think we have to give up the idea that the poets among us will surface and make their voices heard with the help of the Arts Council. If we want to make films, we have to think about how we can get people into the cinema.

RB: But don't you think there's a danger that *Four Weddings* will be seen as a one-off—that the excitement it has generated won't lead to anything substantial? A bit like *A Fish Called Wanda*?

DB: Yes, it's a problem. We have a success and then we blow it. But the biggest danger of blowing it, I think, is in thinking we can copy the Americans.

RB: You're right, we can't compete with the Americans. There isn't the money, but more importantly there isn't the landscape for that kind of film. In a British thriller the use of guns still seems unreal.

DB: That's why we made the decision not to use guns in *Shallow Grave*. There is something wholly false about fellows with guns in Britain. There are still very few guns around. For a British film we have to be clever in the way Richard Curtis was with his script for *Four Weddings*: through Mr. Bean and Blackadder, he has built up a relationship with his audience.

RB: I don't want to give the impression of being elitist, but I am a little skeptical of this idea of crowd-pleasing. If there's art involved in film-making, isn't one of the artist's responsibilities to be in tension with the audience?

DB: No, no, no. Art is always an important element, but the thing about identifying your audience is that you've got to keep ahead of them. Audiences want a strong, driving narrative. You weren't surprised by the ending of *Shallow Grave*, but most of our audiences are.

RB: I would love to be in a position where I was working with a director with whom I shared a vision and interests, the kind of relationship Loach and Allen have built up. Have you found that kind of relationship with John Hodge?

DB: Yes, and the three of us hope to work together again. We're trying to adapt a book called *Train Spotting*, an extraordinary novel by Irvin Welsh. Again, it's set in Edinburgh, but it shows a very different side of Edinburgh life. It's about a group of people who happen to be deeply involved in heroin addiction, but it's a comedy—it's very, very funny. Then John has just finished an original script called *A Life Less Ordinary*, which we hope to make after that.

To work collaboratively you have to sacrifice quite a lot of yourself. One view of film-making is of a massive ego crushing everything else in pursuit of some extraordinary vision. I don't subscribe to that. In fact, it has improved my work tenfold to share it with others and to sacrifice quite a lot of my own vision. But it's difficult to find people to work with in that way.

If you were going to make a film about three professional, intelligent, affluent people living in a flat together, would you make a slow, painful film? I don't want to talk about what lies behind *Shallow Grave* because then I would be trying to set myself up as one of those people I despise—people who believe they've got a message, and other people need this message to make better lives for themselves.

RB: There's difference between a message and an idea.

The Boys Are Back in Town

Geoffrey Macnab/1996

From *Sight and Sound* 6, no. 2 (1996). Copyright British Film Institute. Reprinted with permission.

Few British movies begin quite as arrestingly as *Trainspotting*. Iggy Pop's "Lust for Life" is pounding away on the soundtrack. With store detectives in hot pursuit, Renton is running down Edinburgh's Princes Street, that cynosure for shoppers, tourists, and tartan-and-shortbread connoisseurs. His face, seen in big close-up, is sporting a wry smile. He's enjoying himself. As he sprints, there's a voice-over, extracted directly from the novel. It's the sheer, untrammeled energy of the scene that impresses. "From the team that brought you *Shallow Grave*," trumpets the publicity. Given the success of that movie (it made over £5 million at the domestic box office), you might have expected the team to play it safe: to take the large budgets being offered to them by Hollywood or to set up shop at Pinewood or Shepperton. Instead, they chose to make an adaptation of Welsh's scabrous lowlife novel. They had a disused Glasgow cigarette factory as their homemade studio. The shooting schedule (seven weeks) was tight. There wasn't that big a budget. But the very constraints they imposed on themselves ensured the film's vitality. They seemed to relish the tension: "It's like trying to keep plates in the air, everything is always slightly out of control," as Danny Boyle puts this.

Channel 4 provided development funds for the script in early 1994, before *Shallow Grave* had even been released. In the end, they pumped more money (£1.7 million) into *Trainspotting*, the first film they've ever fully financed, than into any other single movie in their history. Not that it was an especially risky investment. At the time of writing, the film has already made in excess of £2 million in pre-sales alone. The arrangement was also one that suited the film-makers. "We feel very strongly that we want them involved. Not so much from the financial point of view (we were offered much more money elsewhere) but from a creative point of view."

The three key members of the team were once again Danny Boyle (director), Andrew Macdonald (producer), and John Hodge (scriptwriter). I interviewed them together in a little room above their production offices in Noel Street, deep in the heart of Soho filmland. They were in a confident mood, happy that the film had received a certificate without the BBFC asking for cuts, and also optimistic about its chances of being in competition at Cannes in the summer.

Geoffrey Macnab: Somebody who saw the film suggested to me that it reminded him of the Richard Lester Beatles movies. There's a lot of running and jumping going on.

Andrew Macdonald: We looked at a few of those sixties' films when we were thinking about the montage scene in London. We tried to steal some ideas. From films like *A Clockwork Orange* or *Alfie*. I think that was the last period when Britain actually made films about contemporary subjects that were exciting and impactful, and actually meant something to British audiences.

Macnab: Could you say something about the opening sequence with McGregor in close-up, running from the store detectives? It's a very arresting beginning, not really in the book.

John Hodge: There is a reference to shoplifting in the book, when Renton gets caught shoplifting and runs along the street. I thought that was an attractive opening image. I looked at other possible opening scenes. They were all kind of static or too complicated. But that one's very direct and very simple. It's just straight into the action.

Danny Boyle: But there was a very important shift. John's original opening was going to be silent. But quite near the end of the script process John shifted the monologue which goes with the opening. He shifted that from the middle to the front. And then we all felt the script began to take off. It gave us tremendous confidence.

Hodge: The whole monologue seemed to summarize Renton's attitude, his credo. His decision not to want any of these things that are being offered to him, certainly at the start of the film.

Macnab: In the film, that scene is like something out of *Gravity's Rainbow*. He disappears headfirst down the toilet and swims into a sea. It's not like that in the book. Did you make many changes along these lines?

Hodge: No, there are just a few moments like that. One reason I did that was I wanted to show, early in the film, that this is not a realist, gritty drama. I wanted people to feel they are watching something different. Anyway, to do it very realistically would be unwatchable. You see this dirty toilet you know is full of excrement. But for me, this moment was symbolic. How much are you prepared to do to get opium? Are you prepared to submerse yourself in the toilet?

Macnab: There's so much slang and vernacular stuff in the book. You've kept some of that. But you've also made changes and toned it down.

Hodge: I tried to keep as much as possible. When you read the book, you can go back as often as you like to decipher it. But you don't have that luxury with the film. Everything is exposed to the audience once only. And it's not necessarily an audience that speaks "Scottish." So some of the slang had to be watered down, basically.

Macnab: As for the milieu, the heroin subculture is quite a leap from the gentrified New Town Edinburgh of *Shallow Grave*.

Boyle: The appeal of the book wasn't just the heroin aspect. One of the appeals of the book to me was that it seemed as if it was speaking about drugs in general. That's something society fails to address. We're still stuck in the seventies in terms of attitudes to drugs. In the late eighties and early nineties, society changed. The use of drugs massively increased. There's still this stigma attached to it. The people who are actually drug-users may actually pay lip service to that general consensus, but they know that their own experience is different. We did a lot of research. The initial research we did, which was among present-day heroin addicts in Scotland, was very depressing. You realize that nobody would go and see a film about that. And also that wasn't the approach that Welsh took. For all the veneer of realism, the gruesomeness and repulsiveness is used stylistically. The book is exciting, funny, and dangerous in a way that a severe heroin addict's life isn't. The book has that vibrancy which connects with why people take drugs. It blazes away with this sense of experiment and risk.

Macnab: And did this extend to your formal approach? If you think of other filmic representations of drug-taking, things like *The Man with the Golden Arm* or *Christiane F.*, they're relentlessly gloomy, doom-laden films.

Macdonald: That wasn't the kind of film that we wanted to make—

Boyle (interrupting): That isn't what drugs are about. When you take drugs, you have a fucking great time—unless you're very unlucky. We wanted the film to capture that. There's half of the film which obviously is considerably darker. If you prolong your experience with drugs, your life will darken. The film doesn't try to hide that. But it also doesn't try to hobble along with the moral consensus.

Hodge: There's such a difference in tone between the two halves of the film. In the first half, a lot of what takes place has nothing to do with heroin. It's shooting dogs in the park, job interviews, that sort of thing. It's mainly fun. We wouldn't have wanted to keep that tone going through the second half, which is mainly to do with time spent on heroin. We wanted to contrast the exuberance of what happened before with the downside of what came later.

Macnab: Did you view the film as a kind of sequel, at least in stylistic terms, to *Shallow Grave*?

Macdonald: It's the same designer, director, cameraman who actually put the images up there. We made a very early decision (it was one of the things that attracted us to the book) that it wasn't realism and we didn't want to do it like that. We didn't want to make the film on location. I believe that to make a film of this scale on location, even if it wasn't on a grim housing scheme, is almost impossible. I've seen so many other small British films fail because they only have six weeks shooting, and if it rains, it rains. The only way we could make it—especially with 230 scenes in the film—was to do as much of it in the studio as we could. That decision, stylistically, affects the rest of the film.

Boyle: If we had a chance to go back to *Trainspotting*, we'd make even more of it in the studio. Realism is Britain's trademark in terms of television drama and film. We've made this choice to dampen ourselves down so that sex and colors are not something to be celebrated. And if you go out on the street, we're such a small country architecturally and geographically that it's very difficult to create a sense of myth. It's very difficult actually to expand—to create a space big enough for the cinema screen. That's why television has evolved so well. We see so much of our country shown on television and it fits very nicely. It's very difficult to show those same images, to expand them, for the big screen. Unless, of course, if you can do it in the studio and build your own world, and you've got a good designer (which we have) and you can use colors, space, and movement that is not natural in British flats and houses and streets. The problem with Britain, as far as interiors are concerned, is getting shots of people you can go full length on. That's why our instinct is always to build the room so we can do that. The big screen is about trying to show people's physicality rather than just their faces.

Hodge: In writing terms, I have this fear of scenes which involve British streets, or interaction with a lot of people in a normal setting. I always like to think of characters isolated. So that's like when Renton comes out of the pub after the trial and he has to get to Swanney's to take the drugs. I was thinking, how can I get him there? Are we going to have to see him on the bus or on the street. I thought, no, I can't be bothered with that. We'll just have him jumping off the wall and running there because to me, that's more natural.

Macnab: Can you say something about the music, for instance your ironic use of "Perfect Day" by Lou Reed in the overdose sequence? Was it easy to get permissions?

Macdonald: It was a nightmare. It is still going on. All the contemporary British bands we were able to meet somehow through *Shallow Grave* and through the book—Blur, Primal Scream, Elastica—they all did it for the same price, no matter what the length of the track. I tried to tell them there's no fucking way you can have "Perfect Day." It's going to cost a million dollars. It was the editor who put the music there and cut the images to it. He's the one with the real ear. That's what he is so brilliant at.

Boyle: What we were talking about regarding Britain, the light, the streetlife, the feeling of it being more to do with morality than imagination: one of the things that you don't get that in is pop music.

Macnab: So is this the first Britpop film?

Boyle: Well, we didn't want the film to stop, like the book, in the eighties. We wanted to bridge across to now. So we decided to use the music. It's also there in Welsh's writing, not just in *Trainspotting*, but in *Acid House* and *Marabou Stork Nightmare*. We wanted to go through dance music and emerge into what is currently sweeping the nation, if not the world—Britpop. So it has got an appeal to people who go to the cinema.

Macnab: How much license did you give the actors? Take Spud's job interview while on speed, for example.

Boyle: A lot of that was based around Ewen's performance. Ewen Bremner is a unique performer. If you try to do anything with their performance, like give them notes, you just ruin it. They're freewheeling spirits. If you get all the ground set out right, you just let him have a go at it. We shot in a series of different sizes, but just let him do the scene straight through and waste film. Just let him fire away at it. We wanted him in a big open space. We imprisoned him in a chair at the far end of the room. His whole body language, if you know him as a performer, is about getting out of that chair. You don't want to say to him, don't move so much, we can't hold focus on you. It's restricting him. You want an actor like him to be free to do what he wants. So you shoot it wide and he can jump about as much as he likes. We shaped the film around the actors. You have a big screen. And the wonderful thing about a big screen is that people can select. That's the wonderful thing about Tarantino which nobody says—that he lets you select what you watch. He lets the actors get on with it rather than shape everything all the time.

Macnab: A criticism leveled at the book is that it lacks strong women characters and that there's a vein of machismo running through it. Was this a problem for you?

Hodge: Yes, we discussed it. The book is very much about a gang of boys. There are a couple of token chapters from a woman's point of view.

Macdonald: Which somehow aren't the best chapters of the book anyway.

Boyle: John wrote some more scenes for the main girl, the school girl which we filmed, but which were cut. She was very good in the scenes. The scenes were very good in themselves. But they didn't quite live in the film. When you get down to honing the film, cutting and cutting it, they drop out—they're not quite as organized as the scenes with the boys.

Macdonald: We probably tried a bit too hard to use them to define her. We probably worried about it too much.

Boyle: It's quite interesting, all that boy's own stuff. We deliberately put in a scene where she looks at his dick and says, "not a lot," to balance what some people see as a misogyny in it. The boy's own thing is what the title is really about. It's this thing about lists in the film. Everybody talks in lists. They're always listing their achievements—it's a mentality, an attempt to try to get a fix on the world. Tarantino is an absolute trainspotter. It's a very male thing. You can't get a grip on the world because it's spiraling, escalating out of control. So you do it through small things. It's a typical male attitude. It's the Nick Hornby in us all, trying to keep a hold on things.

Macnab: Do you see it as a Scottish film? After all, there's no Scottish funding.

Macdonald: Somebody said to me that in France, *Shallow Grave* was sold as a "Scottish thriller." It was very popular. In France, they think Scotland is terribly exotic. I suppose I feel, because I live in London now, that *Trainspotting* is a British film. As a producer, I hope it appeals to people in London. It has to appeal to people in London. Otherwise, we're fucked. In terms of the accents and all that sort of thing, we wanted everybody to be able to understand it. We wanted it to play in the UCIs and for people to go and see it. I still don't feel it will be as popular as *Shallow Grave*. There's a line to cross, namely heroin, and people will feel that it's not a pleasant subject. In a way, I still see it as a Scottish film. I think, great, it may be the first ever Scottish film in competition at Cannes. [John Hodge has to leave for lunch]

Macnab: Many of the football and sectarian references in the book were taken out. Are you worried that shooting in the controlled environment of the studio you've lost any sense of local identity? A lot of people were very protective about the book, and there's a sense that you've taken it away from them.

Macdonald: Oh yeah. There will be lots of people like that. But then it's not just Edinburgh. It's Leith versus Edinburgh, it's Hibs versus Hearts. It's all that stuff. Our approach was determined by the actors as much as anything else. We could have gone a different way, taken real kids from the estates. It was a stylistic choice not to.

Boyle: It's interesting, that. Looking at the book, you think: should we pick real kids and do it that way? You think, could kids on the street perform these scenes, even as they're written? And they can't. They're not scenes written down by a tape recorder of real things happening in a room. They're highly stylized performance scenes which Welsh has chosen to use to illustrate characters. And you need actors for that. Choices like that push you toward a slightly stylized approach which eschews the detailed "this is Leith, this is no. 23 in the street" approach. But, of course, somebody like Ken Loach would go for a different approach. We always said that Loach would make a really interesting film of this book. It would be very different.

Macnab: Even in the most horrific scenes, there's always the sense of dark humor. Was this something intentional? That you were never going to let matters get too grim?

Boyle: I hope they get horrifically grim. We just didn't want to go into that usual drug world where things are so appalling that you can't even watch it. It just wears you down. We wanted the film to have a vibrancy—a humor, an outrageousness, we always wanted it to be larger than life really. You can get away with so much with humor, smuggle so much in.

Macnab: There's always this sense of class tension in the book which seems slightly less pronounced in the film.

Macdonald: I didn't really notice it much in the book. It's the characters that grab your attention. You don't really worry about the outside world.

Boyle: You talk about class. Class is such a fucking nightmare in this country. Particularly in terms of *Sight and Sound* and something like that. One of the really interesting things in the book I found was that the characters went everywhere in taxis. And I remember saying that to Andrew, "Fuck me, they go everywhere in cabs." That is one of the wonderfully contradictory things about the book. The really interesting thing about class is not how it is defined. As soon as it is defined, people slip away from it. People who are really experiencing hardship or are affected by budget, they want to get out of their class, and they find ways of slipping their class. If they've got cash, they spend it on cabs. They spend half of it on a cab and the other half of it on heroin or smack. It's things like that. You go with that spirit in the book. The book isn't an examination of class. Anybody who wants to make it out to be that has their own particular axe to grind. It's a much more interesting book than that.

Macnab: The end of the film, where the four characters have the bag of money. It is in the book, but it's very close to the basic situation of *Shallow Grave.*

Macdonald: John Hodge manages to twist it round to his agenda. Like any writer would. He managed to make it about friendship and betrayal. That's what the film is about. Not heroin. That's what you should compare it to if you're writing for *Sight and Sound. I Vitteloni* or *Diner.* It's basically about their friendship and how Renton has to escape from it, to get away, in order to survive.

Macnab: There's something quite entrepreneurial about Renton.

Boyle: But that's Irvine Welsh. You learn a bit about Irvine and Irvine is an entrepreneur. Those things about Renton in the book were true. Irvine went to be an estate agent. He bought himself a flat to benefit from the property boom. That's what is interesting about class. If you come with this blinkered idea about the way the world is organized, you'll think this can't be true. I know this guy. He's a working-class hero. But when you actually get to find out about him, you realize he doesn't quite fit that pattern. He squirms out of that. We obviously tried to reflect that in Renton. One of the things that keep people in their background is their friends, if they stay loyal to their friends. The people I grew up with are all still in Radcliffe, where I come from, near Manchester. They're all still there. And some of them are a lot brighter than me. But they stayed there, they stayed friends—and I got out. I left. And that's what Renton does. You have to do that—to break with people like Begbie. He uses the money as a catalyst to get out of there. He knows Begbie will chop his hands off if he ever goes back. That's an interesting thing about class, your own private relationship with it, what you do with it. Not just "it" as a monumental force controlling everyone.

Macnab: In *Shallow Grave*, you were going for all those dark red colors. What was the color scheme here? What was the look you wanted?

Macdonald: There was a lot of stuff about the floor. We wanted the camera low.

Boyle: It's very difficult to get a 35mm camera down there and operate it. It means that you've got to have ceilings. It means that you see the floor and the ceilings. You realize that that is why most things aren't shot like that. It takes too much time. But we had a cameraman who was prepared to indulge these fantasies we had about the camera wriggling across the floor. You've got to have an organic reason. The reason was they were going to end up on the floor. That's where the characters are coming to. That's where they want to be. Oblivion is just to fall over and not feel it. The book's like that—they've got that desire just to fall over. The colors? We talked a lot about Francis Bacon's colors.

Macdonald: Purples—we found a great wallpaper shop. You know the trainspotting wallpaper in Renton's childhood room. There was a shop in Paisley that had all these amazing wallpapers left over from God knows when. I'm sure the film is going to herald a big revival in wallpaper.

Trainspotters

Monika Maurer/1996

From *The Richmond Review*, 1996. Reprinted with permission.

Andrew Macdonald is in the Groucho Club, introducing his team to me. "I lie on the phone," he says with a chuckle, then points at Danny Boyle. "He shouts at actors, and [indicating John Hodge] he writes scripts in his bedroom." The three of them—producer, director, writer—dissolve into giggles at a flippant remark which belies their position as the potential saviors of British Cult Film, the U.K.'s answer to A Band Apart, makers of *Pulp Fiction*.

Last year, they produced *Shallow Grave*, a black comedy which came from nowhere and left its audience looking at their flatmates in a different light. This year, their production company, Figment Films, is the force behind *Trainspotting*, the most exciting film about British youth since *Quadrophenia*.

Based on Irvine Welsh's cult novel about heroin junkies in Edinburgh, *Trainspotting* is a fantastic ride and a bad trip rolled into one. Ewan McGregor, one of the U.K.'s hottest young talents, plays skag-addled anti-hero Mark Renton, hanging out with a group of mates, shooting up and shooting their loads. Fuelled by a soundtrack provided by the best of British—people's band Pulp, ambient stormers Leftfield, and a crooning Damon Albarn, who wrote a song especially for the film—*Trainspotting* leaves you buzzing, high on cinema. A superb depiction of that surreal hallucination known as urban living, it's also a great kick up the arse for the British film industry.

"Cinema is a popular medium," insists Boyle, leaning forward to emphasize his point. "We have to make more idiosyncratic films, but that needn't eschew popularity."

Their film sidesteps the bleakness of Welsh's novel, and concentrates instead on its black and cynical sense of humor. In fact, for the first forty minutes, it's a laugh-a-minute comedy, more *Carry On* than *Christiane F.* When it kicks in, getting intimate with needles, a dead baby, and toxoplasmosis, it hits hard.

So did they think about toning it down? "Oh God, no. No!" asserts Boyle immediately. "All the traditional information about heroin is there. It's just used in a form that is going to get people into the cinema to listen to it rather than repel them. We wanted to be honest about heroin, so the beginning of *Trainspotting* is highly seductive. The dilemma was that we wanted to make an entertaining film about something that is potentially lethal, and this is something that people may find unacceptable."

It was Macdonald who read Welsh's novel first, introducing it to the other two just as they were finishing *Shallow Grave* at the beginning of 1994. This was before *Trainspotting*'s paperback publication, before it became a cult classic and certainly well before it was read by people travelling on the Tube. "When you come across something that special, you just know," says Macdonald.

What they didn't know was whether it would make a great film. To start with, as Boyle points out, there's "fuck all" of a story. Then they were faced with the episodic complexity of Welsh's novel. "When I first read the book, I thought it could never be a film," says Hodge. What he did was cut it ruthlessly, honing the cast of characters and transferring scenes, keeping only what the team thought was essential. "If you're going to compare us to the book," says Boyle, "we have to hold our hands up and say you're right, the book is better, it *is* a masterpiece, it *is* ten films in one."

While Boyle is by far the most loquacious and eloquent of the trio, his partners continually nod in assent. Macdonald is self-assured, leaning calmly back in his chair, counterbalancing Boyle's energetic intensity. Hodge listens rather than talks, only expressing himself with a flurry of words when he has to. But they do, however, share the same dry sense of humor.

Trainspotting is full of jokes. Not just literal ones in the script and soundtrack but ones that require a certain knowledge before you get them. There are cameos—Irvine Welsh as a drug dealer, Dale Winton as a TV game-show host (how postmodern), even Macdonald himself puts in an appearance. And Keith Allen procures an extremely large sum of cash in *Trainspotting*, playing a shady character not entirely dissimilar to the one who headed for his shallow grave leaving behind a suitcase of money in Figment's first film. "It's sort of like a joke," Macdonald smiles wryly. Of course.

Not many producers can afford to be this blasé. Few producers under thirty are even in work. But Macdonald is following a remarkable precedent—his grandfather, Emeric Pressburger, produced, wrote, and directed some of the greatest films of British cinema with his partner Michael Powell.

Although this legacy works its effect on them all, Figment is firmly focused on the now; Boyle, Hodge, and Macdonald just as influenced by today's independent American cinema and by contemporary music as they are by the brilliant fantasy of Powell and Pressburger's *The Red Shoes*. Danny Boyle loves Pulp's *Different Class*. "A lot of the album is about Jarvis Cocker's experiences," he says, "and you realize that's what art is really, just trying to write about your experiences as they happen."

"The people who should be making films in this country are in Blur," continues Macdonald. "And in Pulp, and in Oasis. But they're writing pop songs instead of great screenplays."

In a way, it's up to Figment to do for British film what Pulp and Blur have done for British pop. They could even achieve more. Next up is Hodge's second original screenplay, a "boy-girl story" entitled *A Life Less Ordinary*. Macdonald wants Uma Thurman, and he wants to crack the American market. For the time being, however, Boyle says they'll be happy striking the same chord that Jarvis Cocker has done.

"We're not up on a hill waiting for the masses to arrive," he says. "What's important are those who actually commit their five pounds a week to the cinema. Our films may prove worthless in ten year's time, so we've set ourselves up to engage with that audience now rather than let it come to us."

Trainspotting: The Choice of a New Generation

Keith Hopper/1996

From *Film West*, no. 24 (Spring 1996). Reprinted with permission.

Choose life. Choose a job. Choose a career. Choose a family. Choose a fucking big television. Choose washing machines, cars, compact disc players and electrical tin openers . . . choose DIY and wondering who the fuck you are on a Sunday morning. Choose sitting on that couch watching mind-numbing, spirit-crushing game shows, stuffing junk food into your mouth. Choose rotting away at the end of it all, pishing your last in a miserable home, nothing more than an embarrassment to the selfish, fucked-up brats you spawned to replace yourself. Choose your future. Choose life . . . But why would I want to do a thing like that? (*Trainspotting*, opening monologue)

Perhaps it's a terminal dose of Omniplex Jaded Despair Syndrome which draws me to certain types of film. Last year it was *Before Sunrise, Once Were Warriors*, and *Clerks*; this year it's *La Haine* and *Trainspotting*. Wildly diffuse, what these films have in common are the simple qualities of a tight cast, a vibrant narrative line, and an integrity of style and subject-matter. Most of all they're all low-budget independents, and the nascent Irish film industry would do well to take note.

Ironically, it's because of their low-budget design that these films make their impact. They're not in thrall to big studio accountants and therefore don't have to pander to Lowest Common Denominator marketing strategies. In the realm of popular representation this has obvious social repercussions: in Hollywood homogeneity is synonymous with power, and bland is beautiful. Reality bites, all right, but it rarely wins Oscars. The lives we normally see on-screen are purely self-referential; after all the telephone prefix 555 only exists in cinema space. ET phone home indeed.

This is why indie filmmakers are vital to the survival of true cinema. Witness *La Haine* for example: after years of French flicks full of pretty architecture, languid dialogue, and listless love triangles, we suddenly get a language, a people, and a landscape we never knew existed—and with good reason. It caused such shockwaves in France that Alain Juppe ordered his cabinet to watch it. But indie films don't have to be so overtly political to have political ramifications—the medium is still the message. Low-budget films have to be inventive out of financial necessity, and that's their salvation and their power: they have to find new ways of telling new stories, speaking of lives that have rarely been spoken of. In this respect, and before Ireland embarks on its war-against-drugs, John Bruton and his cabinet might usefully take a peek at *Trainspotting*.

Those of you who saw *Shallow Grave* will know why *Trainspotting* has been so eagerly awaited. With a small cast (three and a half actors), an even smaller budget (£1m), and a single set, *Shallow Grave* almost single-handedly restored credibility to the ailing British film industry. Of course we had the anodyne feel-good fluff of *Four Weddings* and the solid costumed classiness of *The Madness of King George* as contenders, but *Shallow Grave* was that special kind of cine animal: genuinely independent, stylishly idiosyncratic, darkly comic—a hybrid extravaganza which was thrilling and thoughtful. In short, a cult flick which entered (and altered) the mainstream consciousness.

The crucial thing about *Shallow Grave* was its tight, collaborative production values. On a minuscule budget it had to cut conventional corners, developing in the process a stylized short-hand and a distinct grammar. The script, direction, acting, set design, and camera all adhered to this grammar, creating an intense and consistent mood reminiscent of classic film noir. For *Trainspotting* the same crew—and some of the same actors—resurrect this style, but to wildly different ends. Whereas *Shallow Grave* was a plot-driven thriller about the moral dilemma facing a group of heartless yuppies, *Trainspotting* is an episodic character study of a group of unrepentant junkies, drifting chaotically on the fringes of consumer culture.

Adapted from Irvine Welsh's cult novel, *Trainspotting* takes some bold but necessary liberties with the original text. The main difference is the film's focus on the character of Mark Renton, who becomes both the central protagonist and the film's narrator. Renton is a likeable, intelligent nihilist, committed to nothing except a "sincere and truthful junk habit." From the beginning Renton makes short work of the sanctimonious posturings of the Just-Say-No brigade: smack is better than sex and has a "great personality." At the same time, with AIDS and squalor and boredom becoming occupational hazards, Renton knows the jig is nearly up, and makes some half-hearted gestures to quit. But given that most of his deadhead mates are users, and "normal" life so deadly dull, Renton can't really be arsed trying to go straight. It's not until a series of major and minor disasters kick in that Renton realizes he has to escape, physically and spiritually. He goes to London, managing fine until his friends catch up with him and persuade him to go in search of the one big fix—a smack deal that will set them all up. But Renton has found a certain freedom, albeit a limited one, and makes one last effort to escape. It ends up nowhere and everywhere; a surreal hymn to life on the margins, with all its manic messiness.

The problem with any synopsis of this film is that it all sounds dreadfully bleak and downbeat. Its triumph is that it refuses to see itself that way, and resists the traditional, moralistic demands of social realism in favor of a blackly comic surrealism. This style reflects the philosophy of its creators, or as Irvine Welsh has said: "People are sick of the kind of representations of the world that we live in as a kind of bland *Four Weddings and a Funeral* sort of place . . . [but] to see *Trainspotting* just as a kind of reaction to social oppression, to social circumstances, is to rip some of the soul out of it and to make the characters into victims—I don't think that they really are."

This refusal to accept victimhood defines the film's anarchic centre, and is beautifully articulated through its main character. For Renton, everything is shite, including the notion of a national identity which is peddled on some bogus fidelity to ersatz symbolism: "Ah've never felt British, because ah'm not. It's ugly and artificial. Ah've never really felt Scottish either. Scotland the Brave, ma arse . . . We'd throttle the life oot ay each other fir the privilege ay rimming some English aristocrat's piles."

A word of warning at this juncture: if you find this speech offensive, stay at home and watch cartoons. Although the language is hardly ever gratuitous, these characters (as junkies) are obsessed with bodily functions: puking, ejaculating, shitting—mostly shitting—and this becomes the film's central conceit; shit as political statement. This skewed toilet humor may not be to everyone's taste, but it's clever rather than crude, and in the context of the film's surrealist style it's strangely eloquent and expressive.

Behind this defiant lack of realist convention however, lies a distinctly moral and traditional tale; despite Renton's apparent amoral nihilism, his journey remains a picaresque quest for hope and freedom. And although the film refuses to lecture, it sets up a clearly defined opposition between pleasure and pain, e.g., when Renton is shooting up, the pleasure is externalized by a coldly objective camera; but when he goes cold turkey the danger is internalized through a powerfully grotesque sequence of images. And again, when Renton takes an overdose to the ironic soundtrack of Lou Reed's "Perfect Day," the filmmakers are firmly aware of their intentions and responsibilities.

Such scenes are typical of this film, and encapsulate both its strengths and weaknesses. When intent and image gel it's very potent, but when it doesn't synchronize it feels very loose-limbed and anecdotal, a victim of its own brash giddiness. Still and all I loved it, and within the mire of contemporary cinema *Trainspotting* proposes a model of filmmaking that is worth emulating, even imitating:

Choose the cinema. Choose Hollywood. Choose big fucking budgets and small minds. Choose ultra-violence, porn, misogyny, racism, and homophobia. Choose boring fucking car chases and sad silicone bimbos. Choose mind-numbing, spirit-crushing snuff, stuffing your face with a steady diet of cynical clichés and patronizing platitudes. Choose sitting in the dark feeling passive and degraded, pissing the last of your dole on the selfish, fucked-up fantasies of the American Scream. Choose Joel Silver, Joe Eszterhas, Schwarzenegger, and Stallone. But why would you want to do a thing like that? Choose life. Choose *Trainspotting*.

FW: *Trainspotting* is being marketed as "From the team that brought you *Shallow Grave*." Is this strong collaborative process set to continue?

DB: We've got a new project which we're starting to mobilize, based on an original script by John (Hodge). It's slightly more mainstream, a peculiar kind of love story with a twist, and it's set in America. The setting is the main difference here and so we'll need a bigger budget—not a ridiculous budget—but we'll try to keep it fairly sensible and use as many of the same people as we can. We'll shoot it in America but bring it back home then so that it'll remain a British film. That's the big thing though, all this fuss about a film like *The Madness of King George* being British, when of course the vast majority of the money for it came from America. We hope to principally finance our films from Britain.

FW: So you're not making *Alien 4* as has been rumored?

DB: Well, we were talking about it and then it suddenly got very, very serious, and we pulled out. It's a wonderful project and the people involved with it are terrific, but the sheer size of it means planning so far in advance. I just thought we couldn't do a good enough job of it, really.

FW: People are going to make some very hard comparisons between *Trainspotting* and *Shallow Grave*. The obvious continuity for me seemed to lie in your vivid sense of a highly stylized space. Is this sensibility generated out of financial or aesthetic considerations?

DB: With any low-budget film aesthetic considerations are inseparable from budgetary ones. With *Shallow Grave* we twigged—both by luck and by choice—how to get the best use out of a million pounds: if you keep it in the studio, then you keep it under control. You can waste so much time and money in Britain filming on location because the weather is so changeable or because the authorities and people in the street are not really film-friendly. And so your budget gets soaked up. On both films we shot the exterior stuff really quickly and tried not to do too much with it, preferring to keep our powder dry for the studio.

FW: This is very much in evidence in *Trainspotting* where I felt the exterior shots—especially the scenes in London—lacked the intensity of the film as a whole . . .

DB: That's a fair comment really. Again, filming in London is an absolute nightmare, so we decided just to do it simply and get through it. If you've got a budget of £10 million it's a different story, but on £1.5 million you have to be sensible with your ambitions.

FW: At the same time though this can be a healthy dynamic—surely indie films like *sex, lies and videotape* or *Reservoir Dogs* became more stylized as a result of such restrictions, and isn't that what makes them attractive?

DB: Yes, it's a wonderful discipline to have in the beginning. But as you develop more it's like being stuck on an escalator that's moving the wrong way. If you stand still on it you end up going backwards. You have to hand that territory over to someone else and move forward. And keep moving until you fall off.

FW: So in other words your trademark interiors will change as you get access to more money?

DB: Yes. The next film will have more exteriors because it's set in America, so it will change a bit. But there's a sensibility and a tone established now which I don't think will change.

FW: Does this sensibility come from your background in the theatre?

DB: Certainly at my end it's been a big influence, and one of the things about doing a feature film was discovering that all the stuff I did in theatre felt very employable again, whereas my television stuff wasn't. What you learn in television is not really relevant to the cinema—you'd think it would be—but the sense of scale is completely different. The theatrical influence is also a huge advantage when dealing with actors because they can often get completely isolated from a director, and that can be a serious problem.

FW: One of the striking features of *Trainspotting* is its inventive camerawork, particularly those strange low-angle shots which I hadn't seen used to such a degree before . . .

DB: That was a big thing which we decided early on, that the camera was going to be on the deck a lot. No matter where these characters were that's essentially where they were going to end up—on the floor—so we should just be there and wait for them. That was the basic aesthetic and we just followed it through. You have to plan this in advance and announce it clearly, so that the cameraman has to figure out how to get the camera mobile down there. It was very difficult to do but it was worth it.

FW: Do you think that this stylization always fits the subject-matter? The critics are already carping on about the merits of social realism over surreal expressionism . . .

DB: It's fine I think. Of course there could be different films made from that novel: there could be a Ken Loach version or a Robert Altman version. This is not definitive—just our particular aesthetic. It's quite interesting really because I think it reflects something that Irvine Welsh teases at in the book, and which he's ambitiously moving towards as a writer. In his later books he uses that kind of heightened reality much more, and what he likes about our script is the fact that we've gone for the surreal stuff. That's encouraging.

FW: It's interesting that you mention Altman. The episodic nature of the book would seem to lend itself to a kind of *Short Cuts* narrative style. So why did you make Renton the focus of the film?

DB: The blunt reason is that his story had an ending whereas nobody else's had really. He doesn't actually dominate the novel that much, although he does give it a definite ending. And I also felt that Renton was actually Irvine Welsh himself, in disguise.

FW: Critics are commenting on the apparent neutrality of your position on drugs. Is it really that neutral?

DB: I don't think that you can preach to people about drugs in the modern world, it's pointless. People just switch off, particularly now in what is a post-ecstasy culture. The experience that people have had in the late eighties/early nineties has shaped a new consciousness about drugs. That's not to compare heroin to ecstasy, but people do feel that they know more about drugs now. You have to speak to them directly because they're the ones who actually go to the cinema, and you can't patronize them by claiming that you know better. All you're doing by that is alienating them, and satisfying a much older generation who need the comfort of knowing that drugs are being condemned. There's a balance of pleasure and danger that drug-taking entails; when you're younger you're more concerned about the pleasure than the danger.

FW: In this sense I felt there was an internal imbalance about the film, that the camera served to privilege the dangers rather than the pleasures . . .

DB: Well, to be honest, I think this film is highly traditional in many ways, and highly old-fashioned in its view of drug-taking. The only difference is that early on it tries to present the view that people do drugs to feel good, not to kill themselves. You've got to acknowledge that, otherwise you're just saying that people are stupid, full-stop.

FW: *Trainspotting* is obviously set in the mid-eighties, at the height of the heroin epidemic, and its historical cut-off point seems to be the start of rave culture. Was it a deliberate decision to stop at that point?

DB: Because some of the music used is contemporary Brit-pop you could see it as being up-to-date, but we deliberately left it ambiguous so that people wouldn't read it as a period film . . . One of the really cruel and ironic things about drug culture is that just when you think you're really hip you're actually out of date—it changes as fast as pop music.

FW: Heroin is currently undergoing a revival of sorts as a result of the rave scene. Given that your films have already gained cult status among the E-generation, do you ever worry that hip flicks like *Trainspotting* and *Pulp Fiction* might end up, paradoxically, endorsing and legitimizing heroin?

DB: There was a big survey in one of the papers recently—and this is something the government should be doing—they bought two to three hundred tabs of ecstasy from around the country and got them chemically analyzed, and virtually none of them had any MDMA in them. So it's all shit basically, and that's what's dangerous about ecstasy. Similarly, I hope that by the time people go through the process of watching the film—as opposed to talking or reading about it—they'll realize that this film clearly says if you want to dabble with heroin it's very dangerous. But at the same time it tries to say that people are not stupid and make their own choices. Much as we'd like to we can't make choices for other people. It's like building fucking towerblocks; you know the mentality: "We know what these people want, put them in towerblocks, they'll love it." And they fucking well don't! These people don't think of themselves as victims, although their choices may well be limited and shaped by terrible things. It's the one thing that Irvine Welsh does in the book, he insists, continually, that we don't read this as being the fault of the mother and the father, or the fault of the housing estate, or the fault of this or that—it's these people's choices.

FW: In this respect what I liked most was Renton's refusal to buy into this cult of victimhood, including his brilliant monologue about colonialism and what it means to be Scottish. It's quite defiant of conventional politics, nationalist or otherwise . . .

DB: (Laughs) Yeah, it's great that isn't it? I mean this film is about a lot of things, but people always tend to focus on the drug thing.

FW: So, getting away from the drugs issue, tell us about your use of soundtrack in the film. Cynics would say it's just a cute way of selling albums in MTV land . . .

DB: Well, it is part of the marketing process to be honest. It is a fair criticism to make but it's also a question of personal taste. It was quite fashionable here for a while to be anti-MTV, that any filmmaker who mentioned MTV was making shite films. I don't subscribe to that view at all. You're not making a film for your mates—it's a commercial operation—but for the people who go to the cinema, and they're mainly in the sixteen to thirty age bracket. You have to keep your audience in mind. A young audience are quite prepared to take in different kinds of information at the same time.

FW: Soundtracks are often used without the great sense of incongruity that Scorsese and Tarantino employ, that startling juxtaposition of sound and image. Some critics would argue that this device has become too lazy and formulaic . . .

DB: To be honest, yeah you sometimes use it to get through bits, but I bet you Scorsese does that too, he just disguises it better. So yes, it is a kind of shorthand, it is a kind of cheat, but the instinct behind it was genuine—not to make a really hip album but to try and move the film along a narrative line from Iggy Pop through to the present day. Some songs work better than others, and it's very difficult to know why. I just do it as best I can, and it's up to you lot to judge whether it's shit or not.

FW: Speaking of which, I loved the whole shit motif in the film. Why is this metaphor foregrounded so much—is it just a result of bad potty training?

DB: (Laughs) Again it comes from the book, it's obsessed with constipation and so on. It's a major part of these characters' lives; they're obsessed with the body as a recycling agent for chemicals, and their effects on the body: you can't get a hard-on, you can get a hard-on, you can't get rid of a hard-on . . . They're totally fixated on these physical, anal details.

FW: As a metaphor they apply this to everything—even Scotland is described as being "pure shite" for all the naff symbols it traditionally uses to represent itself. What do you think of the representations of Scottishness put forward by films like *Braveheart* and *Rob Roy*?

DB: I have to keep a slight distance on these questions because although I'm of Irish extraction, I'm actually from Manchester. So I have to bow to my Scottish collaborators on certain things, and work through them . . . But actually I quite like *Braveheart*, I thought it was quite political—I just loved the way the main character inspired everybody.

FW: Some people in Ireland thought *Braveheart*'s politics seriously dodgy: racist, homophobic, anti-British, and so on . . .

DB: Really? Well, it's very difficult. I admire a film like that because it was made with such obvious commitment and energy to its storyline. Whereas the wistfulness of *Rob Roy* I can frankly live without. But it's all a question of taste in the end: I just hope that people'll like our film.

Train Conductor: The Director Who Dared to Violate the Just Say No Code

Anne Burns/1996

From *Salon.com*, July 15, 1996.

The *Trainspotting* machine, which started rolling as a cult novel in Scotland's slums (passed hand-to-hand at outlawed raves) and gathered steam as a controversial West End play, is now in full locomotion, a wildly successful movie in Europe with raging fires of hype being stoked for its arrival on our shores. But will a movie about a bunch of toilet-diving Scottish heroin addicts play in Peoria?

A few months ago, director Danny Boyle didn't think so. "I doubt it'll do any business in America," he said. Was he prepared to alter that prediction now, after a staggering pre-release campaign and stories in every major magazine?

"I still don't know, to tell you the truth," chuckles the British filmmaker. With his rumpled bohemian look, the jovial Boyle, who unleashed last year's wonderfully wicked *Shallow Grave* on an unsuspecting public, looks out of place in Los Angeles, where he's come for *Trainspotting*'s press screening, in advance of its July 19 opening.

"I just drove across America for the first time, and there's really a sense that people just want to belong," Boyle says. "And of course the film is about a group of guys who don't want to belong to anything—nothing heroic or normal or faithful, because they've been disillusioned so many times. So I can't imagine that it will ever play in Peoria or Nebraska. But I don't know! I hope it will."

Whether or not audiences will line up to see the black comedy, which was the surprise non-competition hit at Cannes in May and the second-highest grossing film in British history (after *Four Weddings and a Funeral*), *Trainspotting* is certain to provoke debate. It remains to be seen which will be louder: the clucking tongues of the Christian Coalition, outraged by *Trainspotting*'s drug-saturated subject matter, foul language, and generally sociopathic tendencies, or the cheers of disenfranchised youth.

Critics have praised the grimly picaresque yarn. (See Charles Taylor's review elsewhere in this issue.) The adulation is bound to trouble audience members who balk at the movie's unsentimental, non-judgmental view of heroin addiction, a perspective summed up by lead character Mark Renton in the film's opening sequence: "I chose not to choose life. I chose somethin' else. And the reasons? There are no reasons. Who needs reasons when you've got heroin?"

Boyle says he consciously avoided the role of director-as-social-worker, noting that the unbiased view is the more complicated one. "In an old-fashioned message film, Renton would be destroyed in the end, because he's a terrible abuser, a despicable person in some ways. Instead he slides away. And yet the nicest guy in the whole film, and the last to use, is the first to die. There is no fairness, but there is plenty of mayhem."

Renton and his friends cheerfully mug tourists for drug money, shoot up, start brawls, even dive into toilets when the white treasure is accidentally dropped. Horrific as it can be, however, the film is much tamer than Irvine Welsh's novel.

"My writing acknowledges that drugs are now unremarkable," said the reclusive, thirty-something Welsh in an interview last year. "As British society changed under the (Margaret) Thatcher eighties, drugs and drink became less recreational and more a way of life because people had fuck all else to do."

The book, more than the movie, blames Thatcher's policies for handing Scotland a staggering unemployment rate and a corresponding increase in drug use in the mid-eighties. Skag use became so rampant that Edinburgh was known as "the AIDS capital of Europe."

The improbable bestseller became something of a badge among British acid-house ravers, a group usually more fond of tripping than picking up a book. And the play, which after numerous runs in Scotland moved to London—just a posh block from the long-running *Mousetrap*—startled critics with its obscene humor. "It goes beyond hedonism to embrace human tragedy, large and small," proclaimed the *Evening Standard*. *The Independent* was less enthralled: "This is the kind of 'escapism' associated with a particularly virulent boil being lanced." The play was also produced in San Francisco, where it was twice extended and hundreds of theater-goers had to be turned away for lack of space in the tiny theater above the Edinburgh Castle pub.

Now America is inundated with *Trainspotting* artifacts. There's the *Trainspotting* script (a good source for those who have difficulty deciphering the movie's thick Scottish brogue), the *Trainspotting* CD, even *Trainspotting* T-shirts. And bookstores are selling out of Welsh's novel, which was finally released here recently.

It all further fuels the notion that these days, it's very hip to be Scottish.

Aiding and abetting the fever is Scotland's remarkable surge in the arts. James Kelman won England's top literary award, the Booker Prize, in 1994 for his jagged *How Late It Was, How Late*. (Like Welsh, Kelman writes in the Scottish vernacular—a linguistic nose-thumbing at the Queen and her English.) Not far behind Kelman and Welsh is even younger talent: Alan Warner, Gordon Legge, and the ultra-feminist Janice Galloway.

In movies, historical epics like *Braveheart* and *Rob Roy* have further fueled seditious talk, and Boyle is a red-hot director. Boyle's career took off with the critically acclaimed *Shallow Grave*, but he also garnered points for having the chutzpah to walk away from a job directing the certain blockbuster *Aliens 4*. ("I don't do storyboards," he shrugs.)

Boyle says he took on *Trainspotting*—and the chore of turning a cult novel into a more commercial venture with a paltry budget of $2.4 million—because the book changed his life.
"It really did. I was shocked by it and how much it changed the way I think about life. I consider it a very important work."

And then there was the matter of convincing John Hodge, who did such a brilliant job with the screenplay of *Shallow Grave*, to take on the chore of *Trainspotting*.

"It took a while to convince John to do it," Boyle says. "Because I think he had a tough job, to turn an amazing piece of writing into a ninety-minute film. It was pretty daunting."

Daunting especially because both the book and the play were episodic sketches, not sustained narratives: Hodge had to create a story line from scratch. Keeping the characters real—neither heroes nor simplistic criminals—also involved walking a thin line, Boyle says.

"My favorite drug movie has to be *Drugstore Cowboy*, because it treats the addicts like human beings. If you're not an addict there's a temptation to imagine them as being monsters or freaks or mutants. But we can all go there in different ways. The book brings it back into focus that these people are part of our society."

Boyle is aware that the film will be criticized for its lack of just-say-no attitude. This is, after all, the first film in years that dares to point out that people who do drugs do them because, at least for a moment, it feels wonderful. And—dare we suggest it?—these kids are having fun.

"Although their world is terribly depressing, there is something very exhilarating there," Boyle says. "The film celebrates the spirit of these young people, rather than the thing they do that will eventually destroy them. It's also about just being young and all the crazy things you do in your twenties. It's not trying to celebrate heroin, it's celebrating a kind of spirit that exists in all of us before something like age, or a job—or heroin—crushes it."

Fame? They Can Keep It

Tom Charity/1997

From *Time Out London*, October 1–8, 1997, issue 1415. Reprinted with permission.

"Fame? They can keep it!" . . . or so Cameron Diaz thought, on location for a quirky kidnap caper in Utah. Except this little indie movie just happened to be the eagerly awaited follow-up to *Trainspotting*, her co-star just happened to be the next Obi-Wan Kenobi, and director Danny Boyle just happened to be the sort of nutter who'd do karaoke Sid Vicious in a redneck bar . . . Somehow we think the film's title will prove more prophetic: *A Life Less Ordinary*.

It can't get any worse than this: In the last twenty-four hours, Robert has lost his job, his girlfriend, and the roof over his head. Several whiskies later, he asks Al, the barman, for the knife. Taking out a felt pen, he draws a circle on the bar. One half he marks "suicide," and the other "revenge." Robert spins the knife. It slops at "suicide."
Al: "Maybe you ought to make it best of three . . ." A Life Less Ordinary (deleted scene)

"My God, this film really didn't work for you at all, did it?' winces Danny Boyle. Sitting across from the director, his producer Andrew Macdonald and the screenwriter John Hodge in Soho's Union club, I make my excuses and stay. It's not that I didn't like it, exactly, it's brash and fun, and sometimes truly adventurous. It's just that, in the end, I didn't laugh very much. I wasn't moved. No, it didn't work for me. Before the preview screening, Macdonald had got up and made a speech to the press. Something about the weight of expectations, how he knows they're due for a kicking—how this is, after all, just another low-budget Channel 4 Film . . . But it's a painful paradox that those who know and love film can't watch movies innocently. Still harder to make the films you dream of . . .

The latest venture from the *Trainspotting* team is surely the most eagerly awaited British picture in ages. (If it is British: the $12 million budget actually comes from Twentieth Century Fox and PolyGram.) After the tortuous thrills of *Shallow Grave* and the drug-addled controversy of its successor, *A Life Less Ordinary* looks like something of a stretch: a mainstream romantic comedy. Well, sort of. Ewan McGregor is Robert, an aspiring Scottish novelist working as a cleaner in America—until overnight, he loses everything. Pushed to breaking point, he haphazardly improvises the kidnapping of the boss's daughter, Celine (Cameron Diaz). She at least, knows the ropes, having been ransomed as a child. Together, they embark on an antagonistic romance far wilder than any Robert ever imagined.

There's something else. "You have three minutes to announce your intentions, to make an indelible stamp on the audience," Danny Boyle told *Time Out* back in November 1995, quoting David Lean. *Shallow Grave* began in a hurry, the camera careering round Edinburgh at breakneck speed. It said urban/urgent/now. *Trainspotting* too was a rush: meet Mark Renton, piling down Princes Street, fast and furious, a foot or two ahead of the law. Get this: *A Life Less Ordinary* begins in a bright, white Paradise. And Dan Hedaya is the angel Gabriel. (Can you picture Hedaya? The betrayed husband in *Blood Simple*? Five o'clock shadow twenty-four hours a day? The scuzziest, seediest, sleaziest character actor in Hollywood? When he slopped coffee down his bright, white cop costume just before a shot, Hedaya attempted emergency repairs with a handy sugar doughnut!) According to John Hodge, Heaven has the aspect of a U.S. police precinct, except for the all-in-white thing. Gabriel/Hedaya is concerned by the love situation on Earth (the lack of it) and so he despatches two agents, odd couple Holly Hunter and Delroy Lindo. Their mission from God—you guessed it—to pair off Celine and Robert.

Three minutes and three movies in, we're getting a good idea of Boyle-Macdonald-Hodge's intentions. To sketch out a rough and ready manifesto on their behalf: first off, most obviously, teamwork. In an industry driven by rampant egoism, this trio has always been at pains to present a united front, nurturing a collaborative group which includes cinematographer Brian Tufano, production designer Kaye Quinn, editor Masahiro Hirakubo, and actor Ewan McGregor. The model here is

Macdonald's uncle Emeric Pressburger, his long, fruitful partnership with Michael Powell, and their equally extended film family. Then, as we've seen, there's an express aesthetic: bold, contemporary, and seeking to break new ground. That said, it's very clear that they look to the fluidity and speed of the Coen Brothers and Scorsese for inspiration. From the to-die-for decor in *Shallow Grave* to the euphoric cross-cutting between horror and hilarity in *Trainspotting*, there's none of that insipid insecurity which inhibits so much British cinema—no coyness about reaching as wide an audience as possible either. Negotiating the deal for the new film, Macdonald took as much American money as he could, while retaining complete creative control. Above all, they have sought to remain true to themselves. Back in '95, Boyle told me: "After *Trainspotting*, which we'll do for very little money, because it obviously doesn't have huge appeal, we'll do an original script by John, called *A Life Less Ordinary*—which is a wonderful title because that's what people go to the cinema for: to dream of being larger than life." Hence this bizarre and unexpected film, which is also patently indebted to *A Matter of Life and Death*, *It's a Wonderful Life*, and the kidnap conundrums of the brothers Coen.

"What's it like in London?" McGregor asks eagerly. Salt Lake City, Utah, is not his favorite location. "Beautiful skies. Shit city," he says, fed up after three months in the Mormon "dry" state (you need a license to buy an alcoholic drink). There's a whisper of snow in the air this November afternoon, but it's hot and clammy inside the suburban townhouse on today's call sheet—the house selected for its architectural and decorative tastelessness, apparently. It's well qualified in both departments. Boyle bounds up, hair even more unruly than usual. "What's it like in London?"

With principal shooting almost done, Macdonald is still exercised by a metaphysical casting problem. It's only a walk-on, but who to play God? Everyone's first choice, Sean Connery, turned it down. Orson Welles is unavailable and anyway, Macdonald will be damned if a director gets the part. Whoopi Goldberg's name is mentioned, without much faith. "We were thinking of making a statement," he tells me. "We could have a European God for the PolyGram territories, and an American for Fox. We'd like Archie Gemmill, or Jarvis Cocker . . ." A year later, the final print reveals their solution: the Almighty has been written out of the script.'

In its first drafts, *A Life Less Ordinary* was set in Scotland and France. By the time of *Trainspotting*'s astonishing success, it had mysteriously relocated to the U.S. for its sense "of scale . . . and power." This is the team's movie-movie, the one where they can write their own ticket and their dreams will come true—the one with Cameron Diaz in it. Half-jokingly, I recount my 3 a.m. theory to Hodge. Isn't it suggestive, I wonder, that just at the time when Hollywood was throwing temptation in their path (Sharon Stone, *Alien 4*, etc), they should make a film about a Scottish dreamer (The Artists), who kidnaps a beautiful rich American (The System), but that she manages to hijack the kidnapping to own peculiar ends (The Movie)? And what's more, they call her "Celine"(-out?)! After an embarrassed pause, Hodge comes clean: "I wondered when someone would put it all together, finally realize what it's all about!"

The first time I lay eyes on Cameron Diaz, I'm not sure it's her. She's squatting unobtrusively behind the camera, as quiet and intent as any of the crew while Boyle walks McGregor and Stanley Tucci through the next set-up. This woman is attractive enough to stand out, but she doesn't have that aura of "the sexiest woman in the world," as *Empire*, *Maxim*, et al. would have it. Diaz, it transpires, is not star-struck. "Fame? They can keep it," she says. And again, for emphasis: "They can keep it. I think it's a lot more trouble than it's worth. A lot more." "I know it sounds crass, but she's an all right person," vouches Macdonald. "She's like Ewan," he declares, which may be the highest compliment he can pay.

Boyle tells me about how he, McGregor, and Diaz invaded a redneck karaoke bar in Salt Lake. "People didn't recognize Ewan, though *Trainspotting* was playing here at the time. Not to this lot, it wasn't. With Cameron, I think they couldn't believe a girl like that could be in this bar. She obviously wasn't a regular. They went up and sang Bobby Darin's 'Beyond the Sea' together . . ." Diaz takes up the story: "After we got through torturing the audience, Danny got up and sang a little tune for the cowboys out in Utah: Sid Vicious's 'My Way,' full volume, hair standing straight up. All the cowboys stopped throwing their darts, shooting pool, they all turned around and just watched this man giving his all. If it could be termed 'a man.' We were so thrilled—we were *tickled!*"

There's a break while they move the camera for a reverse angle. McGregor cadges a Marlboro Light while Diaz reads aloud from *Pre-*

miere, Larry Flynt's definition of love: "My grandfather went into grandmother's bedroom, handed her a flower, and told her how her face looked like a beautiful May morning . . ." As she reads, Boyle comes up and takes a quick draw from her fag. "That's nice," McGregor says, a bit lamely. "A pornographer said that? That's lovely," Boyle with customary enthusiasm.

"Isn't it? Then he goes on to talk about how he was abused at ten . . ." Diaz laughs goofily and claims back her cigarette. Sixty seconds of normal conversation before the director is pulled back into the fray.

McGregor wanders off and Diaz turns to me. "Want to see my painting I bought yesterday?" She fetches out an auction catalogue and points to a modern abstract, a greyish-white rectangle with a circle to the side. "I know, it's kinda phallic," she apologizes, needlessly. "I bought it over the phone." So you'd only seen the painting in the catalogue? "Yeah, but I'd been to the auction room before. Last summer. I'd only meant to get one painting, and ended up with seven and a bunch of furniture. So it was good I could only do it like this—auctions are addictive."

"I just don't see the point of Cameron Diaz," *Time Out*'s editor had complained to me. There are several obvious answers to this, but, to her credit, it's a question Diaz has herself addressed. A year after the shoot, she has yet to make another movie. "I think she's really sensible," Macdonald observes. "It's not that she hasn't been offered work; she's looking for something with a few lines, I think. She said the life of trailers, make-up, being pampered, it was doing her head in. She said she could feel herself changing. The best thing anybody can do is stop for a while—us too."

"I worked for two years solid; I needed just to hang out," Diaz states simply, when I catch up with her in London. "I love acting, but it is tiring. I was tired of making faces. I know it looks glamorous, but making a movie, you have to put your whole life on hold. The film has a budget and a completion date, and you're hired to do twelve to fourteen hours on set, often six days a week. So you lose time for yourself, for your family, everything. I intend to do a lot more of it. Nothing, that is."

It's been a strange career. The daughter of a Cuban-American oil company foreman and a property broker, Diaz modeled from sixteen, left home three years later, then lucked into the female lead in *The Mask* at twenty-one. "I just laughed my way through—it kept me thin, I laughed so much. We models are used to doing what we're told, so I just went with it, had a lot of fun with Jim Carrey and Chuck Russell. I remember I asked them if there was somewhere my parents could get to see it. Duh—in a movie theatre! I had no conception of what doing a $20 million movie meant."

After *The Mask* hit, she wanted to prove herself, smartly picking out supporting roles in smaller-budget films—to extend her range without embarrassing herself in public, perhaps. Almost all of these indies turned out to be dogs—*She's the One, Feeling Minnesota, Keys to Tulsa*, and this week's *Head Above Water*, with *The Last Supper* as the one minor exception. Yet for Diaz, the worse the movie, the better she looked; indeed, American Theatre Owners voted her "Star of Tomorrow" last year. Her charming, dignified supporting turn in *My Best Friend's Wedding*—her first film with a major studio—will have confirmed their high opinion. Even so, her mercurial Celine comes as a revelation. A hostage to misfortune, Celine soon has Robert in hand. When he can't lose his deferential Scottishness to make the ransom demand, it's Celine who puts the screws on her father with a virtuoso display of patricidal phone-trauma. She's the brightest thing about the film.

"Cameron was on our wish-list from the beginning because of *The Mask*," Boyle recollects. "We're all big fans of that film, and it gave her some kind of status, something iconic, which is valuable for the part. Then we couldn't get to see her because she was doing the Julia Roberts film, so I was meeting all these girls who were very beautiful, who they warned us would be stars in a year, and they were hopeless really. What they expect from a script is just to improvise a feeling. Give them a script which is highly specific about rhythm, and they're absolutely clueless. Because they have no experience. They don't come out of theatre, they come out of high school. They look gorgeous, they head straight for an agent, and they make it! None of them had it at all, none of them could play the writing. Then Cameron walked in and you could tell straight away that she would be able to do it. It's very easy to underestimate her because of her looks. Casting her was the best single decision we made on the film."

According to Diaz, "There wasn't a lot I could relate to Celine on, personally. I mean, she robs banks! She's not the typical girl, which was attractive to me. She plays victim, but to her advantage—you never know what she'll do next. In fact, I was totally surprised by what she does first . . ."

As Diaz points out, this film is "driven by music and action and

surprise . . . American audiences like to have something that moves."
I suspect that won't be enough for more than a cult audience there or
here. The film is too slippery for its own good, too British in its humor,
just too damn fanciful.

Does it matter if it doesn't click? Macdonald's DNA company—one
of the three Lottery franchise winners —has theoretical backing for
three films a year for the next six years. So far, from five hundred script
submissions, they haven't found one they want to make. "Andrew has
an option on Alex Garland's *The Beach*," Hodge says, drily. "The success of *A Life Less Ordinary* will determine whether it will take place on
Thailand or the Isle of Skye."

I ask McGregor if he believes in destiny. "No. If it's all planned out,
what's the point in anything? It comes from us. We create our own . . ."
His co-star disagrees. "I don't know how else we would have got here.
Yes, I go to fortune-tellers. No, I'm not telling what my fortune is . . .
No, I don't think you wanna know about stardom. You wanna know:
am I going to have babies, find a husband? And no, I'm not telling you
that either!"

I think they're both wrong. Destiny only works in the past tense.
The present is always a crap shoot. And the future? The future we just
can't know about. Like the man said, everybody wants to go to heaven,
no one wants to die. In the meantime, Danny Boyle's surely on the
right track: do it your way.

A Team Less Ordinary

Ben Thompson/1997

From *The Independent*, October 17, 1997. Copyright The Independent 1997.

A Life Less Ordinary is a strange film. Even its screenwriter thinks so. But then, as Ben Thompson discovers, that's just the kind of creative dissent you'd expect from the trio that made *Trainspotting*.

The photographer waggles a finger and Danny Boyle, John Hodge, and Andrew Macdonald—the trio behind *Trainspotting, Shallow Grave,* and now the heroically amorphous American adventure that is *A Life Less Ordinary*—shuffle into position by a first-floor Soho window. According to the natural order of things in the puffed-up world of film-making, each of the three men should be fighting for a prime spot in the picture, but in fact it's quite the reverse: none of them wants to be in focus.

There is method in their modesty. By submerging their individual egos as director, writer, and producer into a unit which sounds more like a firm of solicitors, Boyle, Hodge, and Macdonald have managed to create an identity that reflects the way things actually get done. "As far as most critics are concerned," Macdonald says, rolling his eyes, "the director does everything: writes the film and produces it as well as directs it. And that's such a mistake. Which is why, when the time came to move across the Atlantic, we said, 'If you want the magic of *Trainspotting*, you've got to take us as a job lot.'"

Within the theoretical security of this all-for-one-and-one-for-all set-up, there's still room for a fair amount of tension. When someone playfully suggests that success might have gone to the head of the genial Boyle, and he might somehow not be the nice guy he used to be, the quieter Hodge quips—jokingly, but with the suggestion of an edge—"he was never a nice guy."

In his introduction to the *A Life Less Ordinary* screenplay (Faber and

Faber), Hodge alludes to Boyle and Macdonald calling him from their Hollywood poolside "to let you go—I mean, let you know" when a tempting offer came in to make *Alien 4*. At the time of the interview, the director hadn't yet read this, but there is obviously going to be trouble when he does.

Other potential sources of disputation are not hard to spot. After their triumph with *Trainspotting*, the trio are, by Macdonald's own reckoning, "Probably due a kicking." And, in this context, the message of *A Life Less Ordinary* would seem to be "Come and have a go if you think you're hard enough." The nattily choreographed interplay of sound and movement and color that made *Shallow Grave* and *Trainspotting* so much fun is still there in abundance, but, while its two precursors at least showed their passports at genre border crossings, the new film careers through them like a runaway Reliant Robin.

A couple of meta-textual angels throw together a spoilt heiress and a Scottish no-hoper in a bid to make them "fall in love." Guns are waved. Visions are had. Cameron Diaz acquits herself much better than generally of late, and Ewan McGregor seems to be playing the same trans-Atlantic version of himself he essayed in his guest appearance on *ER*. No wonder the media scrum on the London pavement outside the film's first-ever screening seemed somewhat bemused. And the puzzlement didn't stop there. On seeing the completed version of *A Life Less Ordinary* for the first time, even its screenwriter was moved to observe that this was the strangest film he'd seen since David Lynch's *Twin Peaks: Fire Walk with Me*. (MacDonald notes that the film's U.S. distributors weren't happy about this, and Hodge qualifies his verdict. "But I liked *Fire Walk with Me*.")

As a rule, the published screenplay is the cinematic equivalent of a Hard Rock cafe T-shirt—a way for the unimaginative and socially inadequate to emphasize that they have been there, done that. But, in the case of *A Life Less Ordinary*, it makes quite interesting reading. The bits marked "cut from completed film" are the ones that would have made it make sense.

So, do the men behind *A Life Less Ordinary* agree that it's the things that have been cut out of the film that make it such a strange piece of work? "The truth is," says Boyle apologetically, "you tend to cut the stuff which doesn't work: you take it out because it wasn't shot or acted or directed well enough, or it doesn't come off the page in the way that some of the other material does. And, once you've done that, you have to justify the whole process, so then, by changing a few other things, you start to assemble a reason for having done it."

The director smiles, wholly aware of how indiscreet he is being. "Looking at the film now, I think one of the good things about it is that it is slightly free-form. If people get caught up in it, they will enjoy the fact that some of it is pretty inexplicable—not in the way a David Lynch film would be, because it's lighter than that—but it is quite free. And the justification for that," he grins, "and this is the pompous bit, is that that's a bit like what it's like to be in love."

Would he agree that the film has a more romantic attitude to action than it does to romance? Boyle smiles again: "That does seem to be a problem we suffer from."

Whether or not people like *A Life Less Ordinary*—and my guess is that a lot of them will—it can't possibly have the same impact as *Trainspotting*. "Apart from anything else," Macdonald points out, "it hasn't the same sociological and cultural joining-at-the-hip." Did he find it strange that a film that was initially perceived as brash, irresponsible, and even dangerous so quickly became part of a ready-made index of British cultural vitality? "In terms of the whole British thing," Macdonald insists, "that was, as ever, a lot about pop music and a bit about fashion, but very little about cinema, which has always been a pretty distant relation in this country."

But wasn't the great thing about *Trainspotting* the way it seemed to make cinema less distant—responding to, and engaging with, the culture that gave rise to it in a way that cinema traditionally hadn't in Britain, not since the sixties anyway? Boyle doesn't think this time-frame is a coincidence. "If you think about it, for such a small place, Britain's production of musicians since the Beatles has been—and continues to be—quite staggering. In this country, if you've got anything to express, you form a band, and very little of that energy has ever gone into film the way it does in America."

"It only used to be theatrical people or BBC people who got to make films in Britain," Macdonald continues. "Films always had to be 'properly financed,' and everyone was always complaining how hard it was to get the money you needed. In America, you had people like Spike Lee, or the guy who made *Clerks* [Kevin Smith], who just basically made their films and then audiences went to see them. But that never ever happened here, not one film in Britain ever did that. The closest we'd get to that ideal would be *Leon the Pig Farmer*."

Thanks to a whole series of factors, including lottery money, televisual enterprise, and the general upsurge of confidence following *Trainspotting*'s success, this no longer seems to be the case. With a veritable guerrilla army of domestic productions piling through the breach they'd opened up, it was not only reasonable but healthy and even necessary for Boyle, Macdonald, and Hodge to turn their joint attentions elsewhere. *A Life Less Ordinary*'s kinetic dippiness comes as a welcome break from the current predominance of the gritty and the streetwise.

The great mid-Western outdoors has rarely looked more inviting than it does in this British-conceived film. "We grew up with American films, which occupy a landscape of their own," Boyle explains, "and that's where we wanted to go. I know it's a bit of a cliche, but the space of somewhere like Utah makes such an impression on you. Having grown up in Manchester, and only ever being eighty miles from the sea wherever you are in Britain, just to go there and get lost was incredible."

The thing is, though, they didn't get lost. What they did was shift their hi-tech cottage-industry wholesale across the Atlantic, keep their team together, come home with reputations and friendship intact, and make a very unusual and entertaining film that might even earn its backers some money.

"The three scripts that we've done together," Boyle says proudly, "they're not like anything else I've ever read or watched, and so far that's been a good thing. Of course, whether it's a good thing in the end or not, only time will tell."

How does he think people will look back on *A Life Less Ordinary*? "I think," Boyle says cheerfully, "they'll come to see it as our *New York, New York*."

Sink or Swim

Simon Hattenstone/2000

From *The Guardian*, January 28, 2000. Copyright Guardian News & Media Ltd 2000.

A young, slightly giddy man introduces Danny Boyle, John Hodge, and Andrew Macdonald—the hottest movie team in Britain, the sizzlers who brought you *Shallow Grave* and *Trainspotting*. There is polite applause. We're in Dublin for the Republic's premiere of their biggest film, *The Beach*. "And as an extra special surprise, welcome to Mr. Leonardo Di . . ." The audience shares a collective palpitation. ". . . Actually, he couldn't make it tonight." The giggly anticlimactic groan is deafening.

The Beach cost $50m to make. Close on half the budget was spent on its star—gorgeous, pouting Leo. Actually, DiCaprio is not simply the movie's star, he is the film. A few years ago it would have seemed perfectly logical to cast DiCaprio in a BHM movie. After all, he was a fine actor who made adventurous independent movies like *What's Eating Gilbert Grape*, *The Basketball Diaries*, and *William Shakespeare's Romeo and Juliet*. Then came *Titanic*, Leonardo won the world and lost his past. He was no longer an actor—simply the biggest star in the world.

The team is now touring the movie before its official release like pop stars. Only, it's as if Boyzone had left Ronan Keating at home. "It's funny," says Boyle, "We were in Belfast the other night and the audience didn't ask us a single question. It was only afterwards that I realized the guy who'd introduced us said you can ask them anything so long as you don't ask about Leonardo."

He retains the flat vowels of his Lancashire childhood, and often talks about the fantasy age when Bury were a football club to be reckoned with. Writer Hodge (who worked as a doctor until three years ago) and producer Macdonald (a grandson of the great screenwriter Emeric Pressburger) are both Scottish and in their mid-thirties, a few years younger than Boyle.

With *Shallow Grave* and *Trainspotting*, they changed the landscape of British film. They were taut, manic black comedies, the filmic equivalent of the three-minute pop song. They laugh at the notion that they had a manifesto, but actually it's not so far from the truth. They knew exactly what they wanted to do, and what they didn't want to do. Macdonald talks disparagingly about victim movies, and says it would be easier for him to name the three British movies he liked before they came along rather than the ones he hated—*The Hit, The Long Good Friday*, and *Gregory's Girl.*

"When we started out we didn't want to make art films. The art house ghetto is an easy place to flee to," says Boyle. "You know the kind of thing—you don't understand this film, do you? It's not for you, it's for other people." He knows what he's talking about. Boyle has a consummate arty background having spent his late childhood glued to Buñuel and Chabrol films in dingy rep cinemas, followed by years directing at the Royal Court, home of radical theatre.

Nor did they want to make mainstream films. They aspired to the hybrid model of Americans like Spike Lee and the Coens and Steven Soderbergh—indiestream, if you like.

The trouble with British film-makers was that they made their films in a vacuum, argues Macdonald. "People were incapable of understanding who the audience were . . . people under twenty-five. It doesn't take a genius to understand that. Tony Blair knows who his audience is. He worked out exactly who they were, and then he went for them."

As did BHM. Such ruthless branding is not surprising when you see the films, but it is when you meet them. As I walk into the room, Boyle is moaning about the macho culture of film-making, Hodge is so retiring he's invisible, and Macdonald apologizes for his earnest nerdishness as he tells me of the 1,001 films he would love to have made.

Critics suggest their work is derivative, that they are opportunists. None of the team is likely to disagree. "I mean, *Trainspotting* is just nicked off *GoodFellas*, really," says Boyle. "It's just a lift really in terms of style. But that's one thing we try to do, we try to own up to how 'indebted' we are to our predecessors." He scratches his recidivist post-punk spikes. "That's a polite way of putting it."

Macdonald says their best film is not as good as Scorsese's worst.

This is crunch time for the boys. Never have they been so powerful, never so vulnerable. Their third film, *A Life Less Ordinary*, was a commercial and critical failure. It was backed by Rupert Murdoch's Fox, which has given them another chance with *The Beach*. But Murdoch is careful with his money. Success is measured strictly in terms of box office. And if it doesn't succeed in America it will have failed full stop. It's also critical because having created a niche in trendy youth movies, they already feel they're getting old, past it. And they don't really fancy becoming a Jaggeresque parody of themselves.

Why did they cast DiCaprio? For one, they say Alex Garland's novel about a backpacker who discovers purgatory in paradise was too English, so they wanted to broaden it out. Second, says Macdonald, "One of the things that really interests us is taking someone well known for two or three films, and playing with his image." It's an interesting rationale.

But perhaps the truth lies more in what Boyle said earlier in the day: "Essentially, you go and watch movies these days for the actors. An audience lives the film through actors, they have to believe the actors. Hence the star system. You have to have a degree of humility about that."

The Beach is an unmistakable BHM film—fast, febrile, and pounding with dance beats. At times the characters seem like a backdrop to the soundtrack. While *Trainspotting* and *Shallow Grave* had small casts and were perfectly formed team movies, *The Beach* has an enormous cast and only one actor matters. Hodge and Boyle have almost been reduced to operatives in the process. And however much they praise DiCaprio's attitude, his professionalism, the way he turned up every day, you can't help sensing they feel they've emasculated themselves.

Macdonald says: "Taking on Leo was the biggest decision we made. It's not known as Danny Boyle's *Beach* or the people who made *Trainspotting*'s Beach, or Alex Garland's *Beach*. It's only known for one thing now . . . and that's great . . . but you know everything rests on that now."

When interviewed as a team, they verge on the insouciant. The previous night at the movie's Dublin launch party, I spoke to them individually, and they were more open. Macdonald said it's a sticky time, that Fox is anxious about *The Beach*. It's no secret. This week's movie trade magazine *Variety* led with the headline, "Fox brass muscles buzz: Studio hype muted as marketers hit *The Beach*." The story revealed that the studio was cutting back on promotion to damp down expectation that cannot be realized. The movie will never be another *Titanic*—though to be fair, it was never intended to be.

In Britain the film is rated 15, which is enough of a problem. But in the U.S., it is rated R (you have to be 17 to see it), which could be disastrous. Macdonald said this was their fear. "Most of Leo's fans are young girls who won't be able to see the film. The ideal audience is young men, but they may not want to see it because it stars Leo. They may get turned off because they think of DiCaprio as a romantic star who their girlfriends fancy."

All three look the part—younger than their years, trendy, the right jeans, jackets, kiddie trainers. It can create a misleading impression. At the party they stuffed themselves into the first obscured sofa. "Where are the celebrities?" asked Boyle with mock disappointment. "Where are the Corrs? Where's Neil Jordan?" He looked relieved he didn't know anyone. More opportunity to talk football, books, and admire the mute action movie playing out in the background.

"We're not clubbers or anything," says Boyle understatedly.

John Hodge quietly adds, "If you had an exciting life you wouldn't need to go out and make films about it."

Boyle has three children, Macdonald one, Hodge has one on the way. "The reason we get on is that none of us talks too much," says Hodge tersely. Boyle says in a way they are similar people, and their values are reflected in their films. "The morality is old-fashioned. I don't think they're moralistic, but the morality is quite old-fashioned." How? "The hedonism that is in all the films is clearly disapproved of, clearly disapproved of."

In *Shallow Grave*, the characters steal a dead man's money and discover it doesn't buy happiness; in *Trainspotting*, the junkies find endless misery; in *A Life Less Ordinary* a romantic kidnap caper ends bloodily; in *The Beach* Leonardo discovers his heart of darkness. Hodge says: "What you said before sums it up. In our films you have a few thrills, and then things go wrong."

Suddenly they're into a discussion about movies that could last forever. "There is an alarming moment when you're making a film and you think basically it's just the same one," says Hodge. Look at the greats, they say, again citing Scorsese—they've also made the same film all their lives.

"The only difference is that you tend to have a halcyon period at the beginning, ten years if you're lucky," says Boyle.

Today, Macdonald is more upbeat about *The Beach*. Instead of talking about his worries, he talks about the challenge of casting DiCaprio.

"A lot of people, friends and family of mine who are not in the business, say 'Ooh, why are you casting Leonardo DiCaprio? He's a girl, he's too young, he won't be right.' And they see the film and think he's fantastic."

"He's very good in it, isn't he?" he asks, looking for confirmation. DiCaprio is pretty good in the entertaining if baggy movie. But this is not the uninhibited DiCaprio of early days. He can't afford to be. If you're paying $20m for him, he has to play to his perceived strengths—so instead of the unrequited voyeur of the novel, DiCaprio's Richard is a glistening irresistible anti-hero who gets the women.

We are walking to the park to have photos taken. I ask Macdonald if he really meant it when he said earlier that if *The Beach* fails this could be the end of the team. "Well I think you have to blame somebody in failure, and I think you end up blaming each other quite naturally. If you don't make films that are successful together then you probably won't continue making them together. Failure is the thing that nearly always splits up teams."

The trio are forced into a *Reservoir Dogs* style strut for the photographer, and they obviously feel uneasy. "You can't expect us to do this without shades," says Boyle. Hodge asks why we need photos of them at all when we could use a lovely glossy Leo.

The experience of making *The Beach* has been nothing like the three other movies. Throughout its three-year gestation, it's never been far from the headlines. There were stories about Ewan McGregor, who had starred in the other movies, being peeved that his part had gone to DiCaprio.

The strange thing is that McGregor, who was unknown when he starred in *Shallow Grave*, is now a big enough star to take the lead in *Star Wars*, but apparently not big enough to star in a BHM film. "Ewan is not the only one who's upset that he didn't work on the film," says Macdonald. "There's a brilliant cameraman, Brian Tufano, who's not very happy either, but nobody cares about him because it's nothing to do with Leo."

Then there were stories about the environment—Leo wrecks paradise, that kind of thing. Not only did the press get it wrong, says Macdonald with disgust, not only did it fail to mention that Thai locals were suing the government rather than the film-makers, "but the papers don't even care about the environment. It's just show business dressed up as serious news."

But isn't that the way the world is going—for anything to be news-worthy, there must be a celebrity peg? "Yes," says Boyle. "It's a big prob-lem, isn't it?"

The Leo Factor

Stephen Short/2000

From *TIME Asia*, February 21, 2000. Reprinted through the courtesy of the Editors of TIME Magazine, © 2009 Time Asia.

TIME reporter Stephen Short caught up with director Danny Boyle via phone from London, February 1, just as his latest feature, *The Beach*, opened across Asia.

TIME: It's hard to ask you anything about *The Beach* without immediately asking the environmental question. Did you wreck the place?

Boyle: No. In fact, we were there last week briefly and were welcomed by all the people. You know, I think environmental problems in places like Thailand are worse than the government will sometimes admit to. In that way, they try to protect the people from bad news, it's like a more polite Los Angeles. From what I know, from a voyeuristic point of view, the common people where we were, students, intellectuals, tend to protest against their government because they get fed a certain degree of misinformation. I think people there used Leo as a way of raising the profile for them, which was very hard for him and us, but we did take a great deal of care while we were there. In the long run, we as a crew approve of raising awareness in the way the local people did.

TIME: What about the Leo factor? For a start, when I read the book, the Richard character he ends up playing was to my mind always either one of two British actors, Rufus Sewell or Jude Law. Why him—pure box office?

Boyle: I think that's very perceptive of you. If I'd wanted a Brit they would have been inspired choices, but then, you also know I could have used Ewan McGregor, but I wanted to branch out a bit and make the story a wider one by using Leo.

TIME: Did you consider *The Beach* a big risk? Did it worry you as it progressed?

Boyle: We always try to take real risks. People have said to me that using Leo was just playing for the dollar. Well, if I wanted to take the least risk possible, I'd have made *Trainspotting 2*. I've been asked often enough. *The Beach* with Ewan McGregor would have been too easy.

TIME: But what is it about Leo that other actors don't have?

Boyle: We wanted to lure people in. This is a beautiful island, it's secret, a very sacred place. If you add to that the young romantic hero of world cinema as he was then, the two were absolutely made for one another. Using his *Titanic* persona was obviously attractive to us. I talked to Leo about this, and he felt his options prior to making the movie were either to confirm his standing from *Titanic*, dynamite it with *American Psycho*, or to use what he had and take the audience with him. The latter was, to both our minds, more interesting.

TIME: Did he seem a troubled young lad to you?

Boyle: Well, I felt he didn't want to simply confirm his romantic appeal. He's embarrassed by how much of a Valentine's figure he's become. He really struggles with that and it frustrates him everywhere. You know, after all, he's only twenty-four, twenty-five, he's young, he's got a lot of innocence about him and he thinks he's more clued up than he really is. That's true of him in real life and when he's acting. I think he's very idealistic.

TIME: Were you ever thinking of anyone else for that part?

Boyle: Well no, but would you believe me if I told you the studio said at one point, we ought to use Will Smith? It's not that I don't like him—I'm a fan of his—but I said hang on, Will Smith wandering onto that beach? Let's be serious about this movie.

TIME: Was Leo a better actor than you imagined he would be?

Boyle: I think he's only just beginning to find out what he's capable of. One of the biggest surprises for me was how much contact you get with him, you get an immediacy which is frightening when he speaks to you or when he's acting. That's not something you just pick up. Some people are born with it and it's just the most immediate form of contact. Even if he's bullshitting, you believe him and because of the mystique of cinema, you'd jump off a cliff with him and feel good about it. Even if it's a lie, you still feel you'd put your trust in him. Some actors can practice all day long to look more watchable, but put the camera on them and it's just not interested. All it wants to do is turn around and look at the other guy—in this case, Leo.

TIME: Did he really eat that caterpillar in the movie?

Boyle: Leo told me to tell everyone that he ate it, but that's a lie. It's a sleight of hand trick, or should that be sleight of mouth. It would have been tough to do it for real as I'm told it's hard to find insects over there that aren't toxic.

TIME: On an aesthetic level, I watched this film three days after *Joan of Arc* with Milla Jovovich and you could almost have had her and Leo swap roles.

Boyle: I can see that. Leo's a very, very feminine guy. He's very appealing that way. In fact, the nineties have been so appealing in that way too. You'd never have had such a feminine guy playing roles like that in the eighties. It's all so much softer now and less macho. Jude Law I think has the same feminine touch.

TIME: What about Virginie Ledoyen who plays Francoise, well known in France, but an odd choice, unusual and rather risky? Did you ever think of a Caroline Ducey or an Elodie Bouchez?

Boyle: Again, that's perceptive of you. I collect books of photos of people so I always have something to refer to. Sometimes I stick pictures of actors in it, but often it's just advertisements and magazine clips. I'd stuck a picture in the book of a girl in a hotel lobby and when we got to France I asked the casting director if he knew anyone like the girl in the photo. He didn't even have to think, he just said Virginie Ledoyen. I did interview a lot of the top French actresses like Elodie Bouchez, but I was biased toward Virginie from the start. Alex Garland, the writer [of the novel *The Beach*], said the most frightening thing was looking at Virginie and Guillaume Canet [who plays her boyfriend Etienne] because they looked exactly how he envisaged when he wrote the book. I was a bit worried about how the idea of an unavailable French girl would translate to an American audience, but Leo told me Americans are no different from anyone else in the world and can't get enough of French girls.

TIME: Why didn't she or any of the women appear topless? Any group of backpackers on a remote island probably would be.

Boyle: We had a big discussion about topless women, as to whether breasts should be shown or not. In rehearsal, many of the actresses were topless. We thought the danger was that it would make the movie prurient and people would watch it for the wrong reasons. There was one big topless scene in the film, where all the women are bathing in the sea, but we ended up cutting it.

TIME: A lot of people in England say you, John Hodge, and Andrew

MacDonald, with whom you always make your films, are like vultures going in after the kill, looters after the earthquake, as you tend to "steal" from other movies. Whom did you steal from for *The Beach*?

Boyle: You're right. *Trainspotting* was pretty much lifted from Martin Scorsese's *GoodFellas*. *The Beach* certainly references *Apocalypse Now*, playing with Hollywood's image of the Vietnam War. It's also got a lot of *Deliverance* about it, the 1972 John Boorman film. I consciously took from that.

TIME: What do you want to give back?

Boyle: Well, a private worry of mine is that if you look at the films we celebrate, virtually none are ever set in rural areas. I know Jane Campion's new film *Holy Smoke* is set in the Outback, but it's damn hard to find a rural film that captivates an audience, which is doubly ironic when you think the only reason we go to movies is for escape. But I think audiences want to escape into what they live in, into different pictures of different urban societies. It seems we only want to see cities. Ultimately, *Deliverance* was an urban film and ours isn't much different—it's about oppression in an urban environment. I'd like to do something rural.

TIME: Have you created something new in this film?

Boyle: I've absolutely no idea. All the films we make we try to do something different, rather than make the same film again and again. I think that's in the lap of the Gods. You make your choices and just hope they work out.

TIME: Do you resent that your actors get more attention than you?

Boyle: Not much. We kid ourselves that an audience wants to see a Spike Lee or a Martin Scorsese film, but ultimately all they want to see is actors. A mass audience always goes to a cinema for actors, not directors.

Smack My Beach Up

Tom Charity/2000

From *Time Out London*, January 26–February 2, 2000, issue 1536. Reprinted with permission.

Trainspotting director Danny Boyle and his team seemed the obvious choice to turn Alex Garland's much-loved backpacker novel *The Beach* into Leonardo DiCaprio's first major post-*Titanic* film. Then news of tweaked scripts and despoiled beaches filtered back from the set in Thailand . . . Is the finished product paradise or purgatory?

I suppose there are rugged individualists out there who somehow missed *Trainspotting* and never got around to reading *The Beach*. In which case, perhaps they never sussed that the nineties were all about the ruthless pursuit of self-gratification, and repentance in leisure-time. *Trainspotting* the novel came out of revulsion at Thatcher, but the 1996 film was a different beast: a hipper, ironic movie for the E-generation, a euphoric adventure in mind(-more-or-)less escapism, strung out on the sheer recklessness of its own high wire act.

Published the very same year, Alex Garland's novel *The Beach* was a cult which spread with viral rapidity to the point where you couldn't take a tube journey without encountering the paperback en route. The tale of a backpacker in Thailand, Richard, who gets his hands on a map to paradise—a secret, unspoiled beach—and discovers a community there, *The Beach* rewrote *Treasure Island* for eco-tourists who couldn't be bothered to travel beyond zones one to five, who'd studied *Lord of the Flies* at school and watched *Apocalypse Now* at least once too often. (There were a lot of us: it's sold five million copies worldwide.) Among other things, *The Beach* is about a generation so saturated with alternative, mediated realities, it just doesn't feel real anymore—hence the need to escape to Africa and the Far East, to find a deeper, truer You in the anonymous freedom of travel.

Fitting, then, that the team who fell flat on their faces with their own dream project, *A Life Less Ordinary*, should pick up on the book's movie potential: all their work is so preoccupied with the pursuit of false dreams, the rejection of, precisely, "ordinary life." Despite the *Life Less* . . . debacle, the trio's credibility remained high enough to secure the services of the most sought-after star in the world right now, one Leonardo DiCaprio, whose rumored $20 million salary doubled the budget and magnetized the world's media: hence all those unwanted—and, they claim, unwarranted—stories about the environmental disruption the film caused to its principle location, a beach within a Thai National Park. There have been other negative vibes, too: the film's original Boxing Day release date slid back to February . . . a teaser trailer showcased before the premiere of *Phantom Menace* was booed . . . and young DiCaprio's hellraising tabloid alter-ego got up everybody's nose. Who was this irritating slip of a boy to come in and displace our very own Ewan McGregor? And didn't *Titanic* suck?!?

Luckily, most of the worries prove groundless. Danny Boyle's *The Beach* is vivid, adventurous, and barbed storytelling, sticking closely to the structure of the novel but offering subtle reshadings here and there (most radically at the climax). That said, the picture's seductive surface doesn't hide any great depths: it feels like a gloss on serious themes, a kind of teen *Heart of Darkness*. With Tilda Swinton as Sal, Virginie Ledoyen and Guillaume Canet as Francoise and Etienne, and Robert Carlyle as Daffy, it's strongly cast but thinly characterized. It should be a hit, though, not least because here, for the first time, Leo is all grown up—a gleaming, fresh-faced young adult. That DiCaprio should have followed *Titanic* with his self-referential cameo in *Celebrity* and then this very-far-from-immaculate hero does him considerable credit.

To discuss these and related matters, we invited director Danny Boyle, producer Andrew Macdonald, screenwriter John Hodge, and novelist Alex Garland to sit down and chat . . .

Q: One thing bearing against this movie is that everyone has read the book, and we all know the film is never as good as the book!

Alex Garland: That's so true! But that's mainly in Britain. In the rest of Europe, and certainly in America, it's sold much less, and it's more of a cult thing. Here it started like that, then went very overground, a kind of mass-market commuter thing.

Q: Did the rest of you backpack in your younger days?

John Hodge: Travelled on the bus from Glasgow to London a couple of times. Seen the world.

Q: The book was a commuter phenomenon, a kind of substitute for real travel, wasn't it?

Andrew Macdonald: That's obviously how you hope the film will appeal to some people, too, so to be honest February is a good date for us. For most of America, and Europe certainly, it's going to be cold and you dream of going to a place like that.

Q: And the film will inevitably contribute to the ruination of this beautiful country . . .

AG: Sorry, but I've got to say, there's something slightly patronizing about painting Thailand as this virginal, innocent place that's about to get raped by the Western Beast. Thailand is complicit in the things that happen to it, and goes out of its way to encourage all sorts of tourism. And tourism in itself isn't necessarily such a bad thing. It's an income.

Q: There is an irresistible irony in you guys going off to find paradise, the perfect beach, and (a) not finding it, having to create it, and (b) the news story that follows, which may or may not be bullshit, about how you've despoiled the beach.

AM: There are ironies and similarities, that's partly what makes it such a good story. But I absolutely insist that we haven't wrecked any beaches. Thailand has so many environmental problems, and here you are looking at this very small speck, and accusing us of things that are untrue. The truth is, it shows what a big star Leonardo DiCaprio is. Even in Thailand, everybody knows who he is. So he sells papers.

Q: This urban myth Alex invented, the perfect beach, clearly resonates. But how do you dramatize its attraction on film? How does it not become boring, hanging out with a bunch of hippies day in, day out?

JH: What a nightmare that would be! I suppose if you allow people to identify with the leading characters, you share their relief and elation when they get there. And why doesn't it become boring? You're only with it as long as the story takes.

Danny Boyle: I think it is an *urban* myth as well, that's crucial. It's born of our consciousness as urban citizens, so it is a fantasy, and I don't think you could take much of it in reality. Even the people you meet out there who've been there for months and months, they're bored . . .

AM: They're looking for a bar. A beach has got to have a bar! That's the beauty of Thailand, it's wild, but there's always bottled water or Singha beer, noodles, whatever.

JH: Most Westerners, you put them on the beach, they'd be dead in a week. We'd all just expire. You want to see the actors panic when lunch is a bit delayed! Imagine them watching the rain for two days, unable to fish!

Q: Tell us about your experience dealing with Twentieth Century Fox on the film.

AM: We bought the rights from Alex with the money we made on *A Life Less Ordinary*, developed it, then took it to DiCaprio and the studio, which gave us a bit more flexibility in making the deal with Fox.

DB: The studio people, they're not morons. They're interesting people who know a great deal about film-making. If you want to make a film with some mainstream appeal, they're worth listening to. [But] their basic notes are to try and make the character more sympathetic. Americans live films through the character so hopelessly that if that character lies, as this one does, it's like an earthquake to them! Whereas we think: That's interesting, people *do* lie to save their own skins, for their own pleasure . . .

AM: They're just more inclined to business, which most British and European filmmakers aren't. And you can see both sides of the argument. The studio wants to maximize, and you want to protect some of the more personal things.

DB: The other big thing is, for them a film has to be a journey of redemption, ultimately. They'll take any kind of darkness if it's got a hokey happy ending; they're mad about "completion," for characters and for stories. It's very weird, because it is a big difference.

Q: We hate redemption!

DB: Absolutely. We don't go on that journey with the character in quite the same way.

Q: Was there any uneasiness about the drugs in the story? There's this vast crop of marijuana right there on the island.

JH: When we previewed it, they all recognized it immediately, before the cue-line the studio felt the audience would need: "That sure is a lot of dope!"

AM: The kids do love their marijuana! When they watch that scene, God! "What did you most like about the film?" "The extensive weed scene!"

Q: Why did you mess with Alex's ending?

JH: It was too gruesome.

Q: Alex, defend your ending!

AG: I like very bloody, bleak, apocalyptic endings. It's interesting what

Danny was saying about American audiences, because I don't think there is any redemption in the book. Maybe that's why it didn't engage there. I think the book and the film are completely different things, but the darker the film got, the more I enjoyed it. I like the idea that you're looking through someone's eyes who's got a more distorted vision than you have.

DB: I must say, I thought our ending was superior to the book. It's an amazing book, a modern parable, but I think it did depend on this *Lord of the Flies* denouement, this terrible primitivism . . . but this is quite a sophisticated society they build up. Everything that happens, it's because they can't help creating rules and plans—it's not a return to nature at all. So I think John took ingredients of Alex's story and completed them in a better way.

Q: I did think that Richard's descent into madness was a problem. In the book, it's easier, because we're inside his head, but it seems very sudden in the film.

DB: Yeah, it does. We had an earlier version, which was more than two and a half hours long, which had more of the community, and more of that. It's not signposted, except that for me what it's about is a group of people who cut themselves off. They're a microcosm of us, because we'd all like to cut ourselves off and live in paradise, and he becomes a kind of microcosm of them. He becomes an island, a secret. He chases happiness, but for him contentment is not enough. Contentment is available on the beach, but is has to be more intense for Richard. It's a modern disease, and in a curious way it's linked to detachment: the idea that somewhere there's something more intense. That's his madness.

AG: And he doesn't start out a blank slate, he's not completely sane and balanced. He's explicitly hungry, seeking this out . . .

Q: It must be especially strange for you, Alex, to have this fantasy turn into a movie?

AG: Very surreal. Unsettling in a pleasurable way. I felt it most acutely walking around the film set with Andrew on the first day I arrived in Thailand. They hadn't started shooting yet, so it was quite empty, a few guys milling around. It wasn't how I imagined a film set, I imagined there'd be a greater sense of façade, but you could stand and see the whole commune, complete. The other great thing was meeting Etienne and Francoise, or Guillaume and Virginie, just seeing them, the way they talked, they belonged in those parts. It's very weird. And the trick is, not to let yourself do any reality checks, because then it can start to freak you, I think.

Q: We haven't talked about Leonardo!

AM: I think he's going to be a surprise. A lot of the audience of the book, and of *Trainspotting*, are young guys, and I think they have a sort of resentment towards him for the romantic movies he's made, and a lot of my female friends—of my age—just think he's a boy. And when they see it, they're surprised he's different and good.

Q: Yeah, you're lucky, he's really grown up since *Titanic*.

AM: I think he's our biggest plus. People resent that the character was British and he's not, and then when they see the film, they'll enjoy him.

Q: Is he how you saw Richard, Alex?

AG: [laughing] He's exactly how I imagined him!

Back from the Beach

Rupert Smith/2001

From *The Guardian*, August 10, 2001. Reprinted with permission.

His return to the BBC, where he cut his teeth on eight single films and the series *Mr. Wroe's Virgins*, is being presented as a blueprint for the future of TV drama. It's also the first time in more than seven years that Boyle has worked without writer John Hodge and producer Andrew Macdonald, the team behind all his films from *Shallow Grave* (1994) onwards. In order to add to the sense of occasion, both the new films will be premiered at the Edinburgh International Film Festival later this month.

Boyle-watchers need hardly be told that this marks the start of a new chapter in his career. He's no longer the Young Turk of *Trainspotting*, and it seems he's also over his Hollywood phase after the bruising experience of making *The Beach* with Leonardo DiCaprio. To nobody's surprise, relations between Boyle and Fox Studios were never cozy; now he seems to have said goodbye to America. He even turned down the chance to direct *Alien 4*.

The contrast between big bucks movies and shoestring BBC drama could not be more marked—and that, says Boyle, was the attraction. "The entire budget for these two films would barely have covered the catering on *The Beach*. I had a desire to do something that would open out the way I work, that would be more spontaneous. The great thing about working cheaply and quickly is that you don't spend time agonizing over every decision."

You also get creative freedom—nobody at the BBC was going to interfere with any of Boyle's decisions. And if Boyle felt the need to reassert his maverick status, this was surely it. In the event, Boyle harked back to a creative source that predates even *Shallow Grave*, returning to his theatrical roots and paying homage to the city he still regards as home—Manchester.

The two films in question, *Strumpet* and *Vacuuming Completely Nude in Paradise*, arise from an old alliance: when Boyle was directing at London's Royal Court Theatre in the 1980s, a young playwright called Jim Cartwright kept sending in sketches of a play that would eventually become *Road*. Boyle, impressed by an original voice, intended to direct the finished product, but decamped to BBC Belfast before Cartwright delivered the script. "I've always been a great supporter of Jim's work," says Boyle, "because he's not like anyone else. So when I got sent the screenplay of *Vacuuming*, I jumped at the chance to work with him."

The screenplay came out of Cartwright's Destiny Films, a joint venture with producer Martin Carr, who had been flogging other Cartwright projects around the TV circuit without much success, despite the fact that the film of his play *The Rise and Fall of Little Voice* had established Cartwright as a viable screenwriter. With Boyle on board, however, a BBC deal was not far behind.

Vacuuming is a bitter account of the death of a salesman, the ranting Tommy Rag (Timothy Spall), "a collision between Bernard Manning and William Shakespeare," according to Boyle. It's a typical Cartwright take on doomed lives in Manchester estates, greed and innocence, and dreams of leaving: "Jim is in many ways a voice from the 1980s—and I think *Vacuuming* is his last squeezing out of that world of exploitation and self-obsession."

As writer and director got to work on *Vacuuming*, Boyle mentioned a long-nursed ambition to make a film about the Manchester music scene. Cartwright just happened to have the very screenplay up his sleeve. *Strumpet* had already been commissioned and dropped by the BBC; Boyle, however, saw in Cartwright's poetic tale the perfect vehicle for his message: "It's a film about the creative instinct. Music and street poetry evolve in a spontaneous, unplanned way—and that's how *Strumpet* grew. It feels improvised, but in fact it's tightly scripted."

Strumpet tells the story of Strayman (Christopher Eccleston, who starred in Boyle's *Shallow Grave*), a dog-loving nutter and pub poet, and Strumpet (newcomer Jenna G), an enfant sauvage with a guitar and a penchant for nudity. Their spontaneous jams in Strayman's flat are overheard by aspiring svengali Knockoff (Stephen Walters), who propels them to London, a record deal, and a Top of the Pops appearance.

It starts with a drunken pub rendition of John Cooper Clarke's ferocious "Evidently Chickentown," and nearly ends with Strumpet and Strayman being sanitized and creatively castrated by the marketing machine. Those in search of the autobiographical element in Boyle's films need, perhaps, look no further. The fact that there's a happy ending when the protagonists return to their creative roots should offer hope.

Strumpet is also, presumably, the fruition of rumors that Boyle was to make a feature about the baggy scene, the "Madchester" scene, or a biopic of Joy Division. "*Strumpet* is a tribute to all the great musicians and writers who have come out of Manchester," he says. "God knows where they come from, or how they keep going, but they're always there. I left Manchester in the early 1980s, just after punk and Joy Division, just before the Smiths—and to be honest it was a complete pisshole then. But all these fantastic bands and poets kept coming along, and they have done ever since. Now the city's reinvented itself, despite the complete lack of investment in the Thatcher years. There are more bars per square mile there than in any other city in Europe."

Reinvention is the name of the game, and Boyle has adopted new techniques alongside new collaborators and a revised artistic manifesto. With two such left-field projects on his hands, the director needed a visual style that would not only capture the spirit of Cartwright's writing, but also bring both films in on his tiny budget. So he shot on digital video—and it's on this subject that Boyle becomes truly evangelical. "It's such a new medium that there aren't many rules. You can make it up as you go along. That really appealed to me."

Boyle drafted director of photography Anthony Dod Mantle, who applied digital video to such stunning effect on films like *Festen* and *Julien Donkey-Boy*. "Traditional roles don't apply so much with DV," says Boyle. "The director of photography becomes the director to some extent, and vice versa. It blurs the edges and frees you up. DV is very liberating for actors as well: the cameras are so unobtrusive that they don't feel they're being watched so much. And you don't have to treat them with the same technical exactness. You don't have to hit your mark in the same way."

Digital cameras are tiny, and so Dod Mantle scattered them throughout every set. Dashboards of cars were cut out to house them; they went on undercarriages, in loaves of bread, and even inside a Cadbury's Creme Egg box. Every shot could be covered from multiple angles, lend-ing an intimacy and immediacy that conventional film could never capture. The other great advantage of digital video, says Boyle, is that it's cheap.

"That's why it's such a wonderful medium for young film-makers with no budget. There's no reason to under-cover anything; you can just place your cameras and multi-cover every shot. It gives you a more direct, naive approach to film-making, which I really like."

Strumpet and *Vacuuming Completely Nude in Paradise* are clearly a manifesto for digital film-making. Boyle's so in love with the medium that his next project, a feature film on an original screenplay by Alex "The Beach" Garland, entitled *28 Days Later*, is also being shot on DV with Anthony Dod Mantle behind the cameras. "All the innovation and new talent in film and TV is going to come through DV, because it isn't expensive and so people are much more open to originality and experimentation," says Boyle.

"I'm in the happy situation of being one of those people who can raise money when I announce a project. I want these films to give a high profile to DV work, to show that it's come of age. In five or ten years' time, more and more people will be working like this. It's the only way we can protect and encourage original voices, like Jim Cartwright The next battle we have to fight is distribution. We need smaller chains that can harness the economy of scale of digital video. Once digital projectors are in place, you don't need individual prints of films any more. We can completely revolutionize the way films are made and seen."

All the Rage

Tom Charity/2002

From *Time Out London*, October 30–November 6, 2002, issue 1680. Reprinted with permission.

We all know where we were and what we were doing on September 11 last year. *Trainspotting* director Danny Boyle, actor Cillian Murphy, and producer Andrew Macdonald were up an east London tower block, making a film about the end of the world. Popular movie-makers always hope to be ahead of the curve—*Trainspotting* is a classic example—but this instance was maybe too close for comfort.

"It was scary, as it was for everyone," Macdonald recalls. "[The writer] Alex Garland rang me—we had this garbled conversation—and we had a TV set on. It was confusing. Everyone felt insecure . . ."

"I was staying down the road in Canary Wharf, which they evacuated," Murphy tells me. "My girlfriend was there and I couldn't contact her." He swears under his breath. Did you keep shooting? "Oh yeah." The show must go on.

A horror thriller which plugs oh-so-sweetly into that fear of bacterial attack hanging over our heads right now, *28 Days Later* opens on grainy images of riot, anarchy, war, and strife—but this is before the shit hits the fan; this is reality as we already know it and live it. As the camera pulls back, revealing a bank of TV monitors, we see a group of primates caged in a hi-tech laboratory. The animal liberationists who free the beasts have no idea what they're unleashing. The chimps are carrying an experimental infection virulent enough to wipe out the population of Great Britain. The name of this virus is: "Rage."

Exactly twenty-eight days later, Jim (Murphy) wakes from a coma. The hospital empty. The streets of London deserted. Piccadilly Circus. Tottenham Court Road. The whole town is AWOL. It's only when he ventures into a church that Jim gets an inkling of the horror of what has transpired—and what lies in store. The writing is quite literally on the wall, scrawled in contaminated blood: "The End Is Extremely Fucking Nigh!"

On some level, there's something appealing about the notion of having London to yourself. This first half of the film—in which Jim gets his bearings and hooks up with a trio of survivors (Naomie Harris, Brendan Gleeson, Megan Burns)—will surely cast an eerie spell over most Londoners; the transformation is as thrilling as it is horrific. The hush of the empty streets. The sun glinting on an upturned double-decker. The buildings become monuments to obsolescence. It's like the city itself has passed away. As Murphy points out, this is a kind of second-coming for Jim, a rebirth into a grave new world. But however complex our reaction, it is wrapped up in a basic wonder: "How did they do that?"

Boyle laughs. "I was the same watching *The Omega Man*. But now I know: you get up very early in the morning, and you hold the traffic back. Simple! This is why I wanted to shoot on digital video. You can't close a street for filming in London, but you can ask people to wait for a minute or two. And if shoot it on six or seven cameras, you can get enough angles to build up a sense of movement through the city, rather than just a portrait of the man alone."

He had followed up *The Beach* with two quickie DV movies for the BBC (*Strumpet* and *Vacuuming Nude in Paradise*), and it was clear to anyone who saw them how liberating the director found it ("we just went mad, really"). Nor does *28 Days Later* aim for international blockbuster status. It cost £6 million and has no stars. "The concept is bigger than any star," Murphy suggests. Say what you like about *The Beach*, but it seems to have cured Boyle and Macdonald of any temptation to go Hollywood.

"The biggest pressure on *The Beach* was the pressure of expectation," the director explains. And that you set up for yourself. It was a big film, and casting Leo, the pressure was enormous—sometimes crippling, to be honest. It was a very lonely experience. But Leo was fantastic. Everyone wants you to say he was a nightmare, but he was a fantastic bloke. The blame lies elsewhere," he says. "I think I shouldn't make films about nature. I just don't have any ideas. I was born and grew up in a city, and I love London. I go to the countryside and I'm absolutely rigid within a day. Having said that, I think *The Beach* is all right. It's just not *Trainspotting*. In this film, I got back to doing what I do best, which is working with a small group of people, talking it around between us."

In essence, *28 Days Later* is a souped-up zombie movie—though Boyle grimaces when I suggest as much. He claims it's because that tag might scare off the audience they're after—which is to say, you and me—though I suspect he just doesn't fancy himself as the next George Romero. "You cannot make a zombie movie today," he argues. "It's absolutely clear looking at those 1970s films, they came out of nuclear paranoia. It's not that people will die, it's the fear and uncertainty of what radiation will do to the survivors. Nuclear weapons are still here, but that paranoia is not the same. So when I read that first scene Alex Garland wrote, and he's talking about rage, I thought that was brilliant. A psychological virus: you would chop your arm off for an idea like that! See, it's not a film about monsters—it's a film about us!"

It's one of the jobs of an artist to sniff the air and determine which way the wind is blowing. With its nightmare visions of an instantaneous epidemic and desperately inadequate evacuation procedures, Garland's script anticipated last year's anthrax scares. Subconsciously, it taps into anxieties over BSE, while Boyle points to wider events in the Balkans and Rwanda, as well as to the social distemper that journalists have dubbed "rage": road rage, air rage, shopping rage, and their ilk. If the press is to be believed, we're all mad as hell. The question is: how much longer are we going to take it?

"I remember at the height of football hooliganism, my dad told me it was all bollocks, that it was much worse when he was going to watch Bolton in the 1940s and 50s. They had fighting and knives back then, journalists just weren't writing about it. But this social intolerance is something new. He doesn't recognize it at all. It's interesting to speculate where it's come from. Some people blame democracy—which is supposed to empower people, but in fact we have no power. Or you can blame Thatcher, who said there was no such thing as society. Or consumerism: because everything is bigger, better, cheaper, quicker . . . but the fucking thing won't download . . . you phone the helpline and they play Muzak at you for ten minutes. What it comes down to is, we think we're more important than everybody else."

In one of the film's most poignant images, Jim happens across a wall plastered in handwritten messages—impossible not to think of the desperate notices left by relatives of those lost at Ground Zero, although the scene was shot before 9/11 (Boyle had been inspired by a photograph taken after an earthquake in China). When all communications systems are down, this is our last hope for connection and reprieve.

"We debated whether we should take that out or not," Macdonald admits. "For me, there was no question—it had to stay. This is what raises the film from being just a genre movie."

Aren't they concerned it might cut too close to the bone? That in a climate of fear people won't want to buy into visions of apocalypse?

"Is it good for business? I don't know how people go with that," ponders Boyle. "You can't tell till afterwards. You can never know. Whether people will be put off, it will be interesting to see." He groans—"Oh God!"—and rests his head in his hands. "It will be very interesting. Unfortunately!"

"I think this is also what makes it a scary film," his producer insists. "I mean, in a city like London where you can't even get around on the trains . . . London doesn't work at the best of times; to think how it would cope if there was a real disaster . . ."

Danny Boyle: A Death Less Ordinary

Genevieve Harrison/2002

From *Dreamwatch*, December 2002, issue 99. Reprinted with permission.

Q: What's the story of *28 Days Later* all about?

A: I guess, very simply, it's a story of a group of survivors trying to make their way to safety after the outbreak of a terrible viral infection in Britain. This virus is so virulent, it sweeps through the whole population and leads to a kind of apocalyptic landscape, where no one appears to be left apart from this tiny group of survivors who make their way north, hopefully to safety.

Now, a viral apocalyptic movie isn't particularly original, but what's interesting about [*28 Days Later*] is that although the virus is sort of based on Ebola—it manifests itself in the most appalling physical sickness—the root of the virus is psychological.

Q: Instead of killing those it infects, the virus turns them into vicious killers—not zombies, not vampires, but "the infected," as the film calls them . . .

A: Imagine yourself in your worst moment of road rage and multiply it by a million—that's what these people are like. Interestingly, the virus is only carried by primates, so it begins with these chimps in a lab. It's hideously virulent and it's spread by contact with the blood, and it leads to a permanent, appalling state of aggression, where the simple sound of a human voice makes you want to kill that person.

So Jim [Cillian Murphy] wanders round London at the beginning and he's shouting, "Hello! Hello!"—and eventually it will activate the infected because all they want to do, as soon as they see another human being, is to kill it. That's the kind of appalling unstoppable aggression that it creates in these people.

Q: You worked closely with Alex Garland while shooting his novel *The Beach*, but how did you end up filming his first screenplay?

A: A friend of mine gave me *The Beach* a long time ago when it wasn't very well known and I gave it to Andrew [Macdonald] to read and we eventually made the film of *The Beach*. Then, Andrew and Alex were talking about this idea for a kind of sci-fi/zombie horror movie, you know, something that was kind of stolen from John Wyndham and J. G. Ballard and that TV show *Survivors*—we borrowed from all that, really.

Q: *28 Days Later* does feel like the bastard son of *Day of the Triffids* and *I Am Legend*. Were you a fan of that kind of classic material?

A: I'm not a big kind of aficionado of that kind of stuff. I mean, I like it, but I think the strength of the film is that we didn't make it as absolutely devotees of this particular genre. I think you hope to freshen up the genre by being . . . not disrespectful to it, but not too intimidated by it, which I think that's the danger of being an aficionado—the rules are there, you know? "We've got to do this, we've got to do that."

Q: One of the best things about *28 Days Later* is that it is set in the U.K., and much of its power derives from images like a deserted Piccadilly Circus, or a red London bus on its side in the middle of the street . . .

A: Yeah, what we tried to do is find iconic images, particularly for London, that did the work of a huge, huge budget. And this amazing idea that London is empty—which is an impossible idea for us all to imagine, because the longer you live in London, it just becomes more and more crowded—is a brilliantly attractive one, you know?

There are certain technical problems with achieving it, but you don't have to have huge technical expertise to actually do it—you just have to figure out a way, a time on a particular day, when you can manage to get an angle on Tottenham Court Road where you can see it without people.

Q: Your decision to shoot parts of the film on the digital video (DV) format gives it a documentary feel, an immediacy missing from other post-apocalyptic movies. Was this an aesthetic choice more than a budgetary choice?

A: There's currently lots of shooting on DV, and there's always a practical reason that is useful. When you're making films in Britain which don't have huge budgets, you can, to a certain degree, do things cheaper or make your resources go further with DV.

Nevertheless I think there has to be an organic reason, in addition to that, to make it really work. Because audiences are not familiar with it yet—mainstream audiences certainly—I think you have to find an organic reason in your story that supports it.

Also, when you do a film that features monsters of some kind or other, you have to be very clear about how you're going to present them. [You need] a very clear way that you're going to manifest them on the screen. I'd already made a couple of digital films for television in Manchester, and I kind of uncovered this way that the camera works, which is a particular way of recording fast motion, and I'd always wanted the monsters—the people enraged—to be moving at an almost inhuman speed.

And the digital cameras snatch at this information in a slightly unnerving way that isn't fluid in the way that you expect film and your visual entertainment to be. It's sort of like staccato, and that was a big factor—I thought, "That's how we'll do them."

The other idea I thought was to hire athletes to play the parts [of the infected], so that physically they're able to do things [normal people can't]. You know, when you watch an athlete actually perform, you think they're doing things that you should be able to do but you know you'll never be capable of. I thought if that became an aggressive thing—if an athlete turned on you—that would be frightening as well. So it was a combination of those things.

Q: Another choice that gives the film a sense of stark realism is the casting of relative unknowns in the leading roles, even though Brendan Gleason and Christopher Eccleston turn up later on. Was this a deliberate choice, to give the lead character, Jim, a kind of "everyman" sensibility?

A: Yes. The star of the film is the idea of the film, really, so we were convinced that when the guy wakes up, you should not feel any familiarity with him other than him being an ordinary person—you know, one of us. We didn't want it to feel like it was a star, or a personality, or a celebrity, anything like that, because it felt absolutely right that you've got to take this journey with this person as though it's you yourself who could be waking up in that hospital.

Q: Rather than Will Smith waking up to metal ships over the city . . .?

A: That was true of all the characters really—that they should feel like absolutely ordinary people thrown into this nightmare. We hadn't intended casting [Jim] as Irish, but we found this guy, Cillian Murphy, and he's fantastic. He's very childlike in the beginning; he's obviously bewildered, like any child would be, thrown into circumstances where their world has changed completely.

He has to map this journey, which is almost a physical as well a mental journey. He has to travel there from this newborn child, literally, waking up in London—albeit with a beard! By the end of the film, he's arrived at some kind of place for himself.

Q: Although it has many horror elements, the film is not just for horror fans. What do you think audiences will make of it?

A: I wanted it to be a surprisingly emotional film, really. I think what we tried to do is take a genre idea and make it a mainstream film that will appeal to as many people as possible. It should feel like an emotional journey, that it's not just simply a series of visual effects—you have some emotional commitment to the film. I think there are two or three places in the film where you do feel that, you feel that connection, as a fellow human being with these people and what they're going through. So I hope, because of that, it'll appeal to everybody.

28 Days Later: An Interview with Danny Boyle

Sandy Hunter/2003

From *RES* magazine (res.com), January 2003.

Director Danny Boyle's latest feature, *28 Days Later*, spins contemporary paranoia regarding disease and viral infection into a frightening tale of post-apocalyptic horror, survival, and rampaging zombies. We caught up with Boyle, whose past work includes *Shallow Grave*, *Trainspotting*, and two digital shorts shot with DP Anthony Dod Mantle, for a chat during the 2003 Sundance Film Festival.

RES: Your new film, *28 Days Later*, seems to mix a lot of genres, from zombie and horror flicks to post-apocalyptic and science fiction themes. What references did you draw on?

Boyle: With all of the films that we've done, we try and take a genre and fuck with it a bit. We love doing that. It helps market the films, and the studios or whoever is distributing the film love that and it contacts a mainstream audience, which is part of the deal for us. We want the mainstream audience. And then we want to blow the genre apart so you don't get it. So the zombie fans who show up for this aren't just going to see a gore-fest zombie film. They will get something in addition, and I think that's a great dynamic really.

RES: I don't think zombie fans will be disappointed though.

Boyle: Alex Garland [the film's writer] is a big zombie fan. But also he's a big fan of the sci-fi writing of J. G. Ballard. He also likes the *The Day of the Triffids*, the John Wyndham novel, and Boris Sagal's film *The Omega Man*. We were not stealing, but nothing can stand on its own anymore—there is always some reference point. So in a sense maybe, we do steal stuff and then try and put it together in a different way. We wanted a horror/zombie film, but we also wanted it to be more emo-

78

tional than horror films normally are. We wanted you to genuinely care about these people.

RES: Is there something particularly appealing to you about a band of survivors escaping the ruins of civilization, which is one part of the fabric of the post-apocalyptic genre?

Boyle: Supposedly the first such film is called *The Green Ray*. It's a 1920s-era, silent, black-and-white film from France in which a green ray, which obviously had to be hand-painted into each shot, was shone on the Eiffel Tower. It puts the whole city to sleep and a bunch of survivors drive into the city. I've never seen it—I was just told of it by a French journalist. Apparently it was the first cinematic example of the genre, with a band of post-apocalyptic survivors. But the genre has a fantastic premise because it allows you to make a family film that is just about a bunch of people.

RES: The virus in the film is carried in the blood. Is there a connection to AIDS?

Boyle: You can't help thinking of that. Obviously, it's not based on AIDS; it's more like Ebola. There's a book called *The Hot Zone*, by Richard Preston, which we read. It's about the guy who carried Ebola from Africa to Washington. It's an airport kind of page turner, but it's phenomenal what happens. And the manifestation of the disease in the film, the sickness, is all based on Ebola with a bit of rabies, so there is a bit of medical background there. But you can't help thinking about it—ever since AIDS appeared, people have had this sensitivity about the smallest drop of blood.

RES: Describe your work with DP Anthony Dod Mantle . . .

Boyle: He's an amazing cameraman because he has all of the normal skills you'd expect in a quality cameraman, but because of his relationship with DV, he also has none of the ego and none of the kind of mythical stuff that goes along with cameramen when they say, "You won't understand what I am talking about," and go off into this private ramble. I've always suspected it's a bit of bullshit made up to protect their position. Anthony doesn't have any kind of status problems. He's very relaxed and creative.

RES: What elements of visual style were discussed prior to filming?

Boyle: We wanted it to feel different in texture from normal film. Because it's an apocalypse, you can use a different hue, because nobody knows what things will look like if everybody's killed or there are no cars. So we talked about having a different texture, which we got with the DV. We would tickle the color of the film occasionally to create a slightly strange universe. Against that, I wanted this enormous energy from those who are infected, which I was going to get through this particular menu on the camera, which allows you to alter the frame rate; things appear to be speeded up but actually it's real time. So you kind of snatch at fast images, like falling rain or a man running, snatching at them in a slightly unreliable way. The idea is that you can't quite trust your usual sense of judgment about perception, depth, and distance when dealing with the infected. I was determined to do that, although there was quite a lot of opposition at one point as it was thought that it would make the film look very odd.

RES: Did you storyboard the entire film?

Boyle: We storyboarded odd bits occasionally for technical reasons, but I am not a great storyboard fan. I know everyone is different, but for me, personally, I much prefer making things up on the day. You can't do that because there are so many people relying on you for decision-making. But you can sort of pretend to know what you are doing and everyone feels confident. But I love leaving things as late as possible. It's very exciting. But the bigger the budget the less you can do—that's part of the pact with Satan.

RES: What were other benefits of using digital cinematography for this film?

Boyle: The biggest benefit, to be absolutely honest, was the London sequences, because we would not have been able to afford to do those on celluloid and not only that, they would have been, in their very nature, completely different. If we were working with a celluloid camera, with the number of people you need to operate that, it would have been either much less ambitious or staggeringly expensive, in which case the film would have been very different, in part because we would have had to have a star in it to pay for it.

RES: What about disadvantages?

Boyle: Picture quality, especially on wide shots. We were fortunate; on the whole we got away with it. When you dwell on a wide shot, the human eye is so extraordinary that it goes to where it is interested on that big screen and it zooms in, just like that zoom in on the video game Halo! If the eye is interested in that picture and if the detail isn't there, it looks a bit shitty. Whereas on film, you can go in that close and there's enough detail there so it is still acceptable. That's the only major disadvantage. I am not sure if DV would work for period films as there is something completely modern about its feel and about it as a recording or capturing process. If you did a Jane Austin novel or great period piece, I don't know what it would look like; it might feel very odd.

RES: How did you shoot the film's scenes of London emptied of people?

Boyle: We literally turned up and spent a couple of minutes filming in each place, but with ten cameras. And we'd choose the angles, set them up very carefully so we knew that when we cut them together it would make you feel like it was rolling on and that you were walking around the city with him and there was no one there. You immediately begin to pull the audience into this strange, new universe really, so when the attacks come, you feel vulnerable as well because you've been lured in.

RES: Tell us more about how the scenes with the infected were created.

BOYLE: My editor, Chris Gill, is wonderful. He has a technique, which is one of the reasons that I hired him, where he edits and compresses time. So I'll shoot you going to that door to open it and the way he edits it, he will get you to that door far more quickly than is humanly possible. For a film like this, it makes you uneasy, and I felt that was a wonderful quality. When you get a good partnership with an editor you then start to shoot with an understanding of how he is going to cut it.

RES: What other elements contribute to the film's relentless feel?

Boyle: Music. We have this Godspeed You Black Emperor track at the beginning. They are amazing. We went to meet them and they were very reluctant as normally they don't license their work for features. They were a lovely bunch of people. This slow, very elegiac start which their music builds from virtually nothing to an apocalyptic crescendo; it was a fantastic template for the film. And what we did was use that track at the beginning and then the composer, John Murphy, took it as inspiration for the end, which has a rhythmic looping track that builds and builds and builds. You are trapped in the headlights, it's too late, you can't get out, it's getting louder and louder . . .

RES: Addressing ethical dilemmas, individual freedom versus the common good, is this an intentional theme in your films?

Boyle: It's been a crucial part of the last two decades of British life, with the individual dominating in a way society can't sustain. We are told it's more to do with selling dreams, which I guess America takes a lot of pride in. But we sell these dreams to people so brilliantly now that we are far ahead of our capability of delivering them, so people become obsessed, thinking, I should be able to have that, I should be able to go where I want with very little money. The reality is it doesn't work like that. You get tension, frustration builds, and violence comes in. Those are ideas we worked with.

RES: Will your next film be digital?

Boyle: Not the next one. You should have an organic reason, where it suits the particular story you are doing, although I think eventually everyone will be working in digital. The weird thing will be the people who pop into celluloid now and again. At the moment I will be working on celluloid but I will go back to digital; I have no problem there at all.

RES: What is your next film?

Boyle: It's a thing called *Millions*, by a writer called Frank Cottrell Boyce. It sounds crushingly dull as it's about the changeover in the U.K. from the Pound Sterling to the Euro. This film supposes it is going to happen on one particular weekend. So the story is the opportunity on this one weekend that the changeover gives to criminals, and obviously filmmakers. So it is not as crushingly dull as it sounds! I just sell it that way so people's expectations will be very low. It's a very optimistic film about two young lads and really, about saying goodbye to things.

Danny Boyle: The Looking Closer Interview

Jeffrey Overstreet/2005

From the Looking Closer website, February 2005. Jeffrey Overstreet is the author of Through a Screen Darkly: Looking Closer at Beauty, Truth and Evil at the Movies, as well as the novel Auralia's Colors. He interviewed Danny Boyle for Christianity Today's website. He blogs at LookingCloser.org.

Overstreet: In spite of Damian, who's a God-fearing boy, a friend of the saints, and a help to the poor, *Millions* never becomes "preachy." Was that difficult to do?

Boyle: You can go through the whole filmmaking experience being careful, saying, "I've got to make sure this isn't preachy." But you can't make a film like that. What you do instead is concentrate on the essentials, the positives: the character and the kid playing the character. You're saying that this is the way he sees the world.

If the movie works, it's because you realize that life absolutely is that simple, the way Damian sees it. It's not like we're preaching at people and saying, "Don't you see it's that simple? Why can't you do that? Come on, cough up the money!" We're actually saying that, "When you look back at what you were like [at Damian's age], it was that simple. And that's not a bad thing." That's still us, even though we've moved on into the venal world of survival and competition.

Overstreet: Damian and his brother see the world so differently. Damian's generosity and compassion has its roots in his faith. Anthony's materialism, anxiety, and lack of trust are rooted in . . . what exactly?

Boyle: The whole structure of this story is built around the fact that Damian is eight. This was borne out by the research we did, by the auditions for Damian's role in this film—all of the ten-year-olds, like

Damian's brother Anthony in the film, have a foot through the door of adulthood, and they're greedy for more of it. You can't turn back at that door once it's open. But the eight-year-olds—all of them—they didn't have that yet. So it's somewhere between eight and ten that it happens.

I've thought about it a lot, because I've got kids. I didn't notice that change in them myself, because when you're bringing up kids, you're bringing them up every day. You're not looking at sample groups like that.

So the whole film is built around the difference between Damian and Anthony and the battle between them. There's the older brother who sees the world as "real" and he's always talking about what's real and what's not, what the tax rate is and what it isn't, and what the mortgage is. The younger kid—he's talking about the "unreal." He's not self-conscious about things being unreal, because he doesn't even think about them being unreal. He sees these figures and he communicates with them, and that's his world. And it's tangible and real—it's not imagined, it's real.

So when he wins the debate, he gets to spend the money the way he thinks it ought to be spent, because they've all tried to do something that they wanted to do with it, and they've all failed. It's like that phrase . . . what is it? . . . "You keep what you've got by giving it all away."

Overstreet: "You keep what you've got by giving it all away." That sounds like the refrain of almost every U2 song.

Boyle: It does! I was actually thinking of that song by Ian Brown, the guy from the Stone Roses: "Keep What Ya Got."

Overstreet: So, from what you're saying, it sounds like we're to understand that Damian really does have these encounters with Saints. It that what you mean? Or is it instead that he's a kid with a really active, healthy imagination?

Boyle: Wordsworth, the poet—in one of his poems he talks about childbirth. You're born from the sea, and as you walk up the shore, you know where you've come from, and you can see your Creator. You can see where you've come from. But once language (your ability to describe things) arrives, you've just come over the brow of the hill. And you look back and you can't see it anymore.

Before the point of language arriving, you're still in touch with your

source. When you look at babies, there's something in their eyes sometimes. They look over your shoulder sometimes, and it's not like they're
going "gaa gaa." They're looking at something. And you look back, but
you've lost it. And you think, "What are they looking at?" So I think
there is something in that.

Overstreet: It's a brave thing to bring up religion in a movie these days.
It was so controversial for Mel Gibson to put *The Passion of the Christ* on
the screen. But that came from a deep sense of religious conviction. Is
there any personal resonance for you with the iconography of Catholicism and the Christian tradition that inspires Damian's imagination?

Boyle: Oh, yeah, I was brought up a very strict Catholic. My mom was
a devout Irish Catholic and she wanted me to be a priest, until I was
about thirteen. One of her favorite saints was Our Lady of Fatima. So I
was surrounded by it as a kid. My mom has been dead since 1985, but
the film's dedicated to my mom and my dad.

But in the film, it's not like Damian is a religious child. Before he
[develops an interest in] other myths and icons that he comes across,
like cinema or women, all the different things that we fill our lives
with—our inclinations—then it's saints, as for me it was, certainly.

I think the important thing about his relationship with the saints is
that it's his imagination. That's what allows him access to them or not.
It's about whether you believe. Some people believe they're real—even
some people making this film think they're real. Others think they're
just flights of the imagination. But Damian is an artist, and he has access to that. It will take him different places as he gets older. So it's not
like he's a religious figure. It's faith that's linked to the imagination—
the power of taking a leap—rather than it being faith in a strictly conventional religious sense.

Martin Scorsese talks about this book he's read called *The Six O'Clock
Saints*. It is an absolutely extraordinary book. The stories are like cinema. They're violent. They're incredibly racy and exciting and dangerous. The light that shines on these people is different. It's like the light
that shines on Travis Bickle in *Taxi Driver*. It picks them out as being
the superheroes, which is what they are—whether they're antiheroes or
not. They're the super figures, the ultra-figures that deserve to become
icons. It's the same process. Movies have taken us away from it in a
strictly religious sense.

Overstreet: You made *Millions* soon after the zombie movie *28 Days*

Later. You've done wild romantic comedies and now you've got a sci-fi project in the works. Is there a central theme or a moral question that threads through the projects you take on?

Boyle: As soon as you say they're about morality, you're heading in that territory where things become preachy. But there is a moral factor to them, yes. I think all you try and do is test your own principles against ideas.

I personally accept that we've left behind ideologies. We've decided, as Westerners, that we've left behind ideological choices. We've become what we are—consumers. And we're all in that race to consume. But within that, there remain principles that you do have or you don't have. And you can test them in certain circumstances through stories, and that's the idea behind it.

I think they're all very moral films, but I wouldn't particularly want them to be known as that, because they're not meant to be. That's like the DNA of them. They're not necessarily about that on the surface level. They're entertaining. I want them to be really entertaining. And I want them to play as widely as possible. I don't want to exclude anybody from them. I don't want to exclude any of the *28 Days Later* audience from *Millions*, although I suspect some of them will avoid it when they hear what it's about. I don't want to exclude any of *The Passion of the Christ* audience either. Because whatever the film's about, whether they're easy or not, I want them to be stimulating for any audience. It's not about appealing to the lowest common denominator. It's about working as hard as possible to get as big an audience as possible to see what's interesting to talk about.

I try to put an energy in my films that's life-affirming, that's redemptive. Sometimes what it's looking at is awful—like *Trainspotting*: What's going on there is awful. But there's an energy level that's running through it, life pulsing away, in ways that are unacceptable and unpalatable. But it's pulsing. And that in itself is a victory, I think.

Overstreet: What's the most rewarding thing you hear from someone who's seen your film?

Boyle: I was in Glasgow. This was after we made our first film, *Shallow Grave*, and I was walking down High Street, and I'd gone past an HMV, which is a record store like Virgin or Tower. I walked past it and this young guy came out of HMV, and I thought he was going to belt me, because he was running at me! And he came right up to me and he said, "[Bleep]ing great film, mate!" And he went back into the shop. That has stuck with me more than anything. I remember his face.

Overstreet: Tell me about the boys you chose for the roles.

Boyle: I chose Alex because he walked through the door, and I saw him out of the corner of my eye, and I went, "I'll be, that's him." When you do that, you have to be really tough with them because you want to make sure you're not casting them just because they look right. So you have to audition them quite tough. Alex auditioned and he was really interesting. He wasn't very good (but you wouldn't expect him to be, as he'd just turned eight). He wasn't very good, and that put off a lot of people. And a lot of people wanted this other guy who was a much better actor. But you don't want an actor—you want a presence who's actually going to live in this world. You don't want kids to have that affectation that's part of being a professional actor—that skill and knowledge.

His older brother is an actor. He's got timing. He knows how to make things funny. He knows how to pause and then say the line. He doesn't have to be told it. It's in his DNA. I don't care what happens to him between now and eighteen, that lad will be an actor. I just know it.

Overstreet: You've worked in so many genres. What's next?

Boyle: We're making *Sunshine* next, which is a sci-fi film. We've done about twenty drafts. It's written by Alex Garland, the guy who did *28 Days Later*.

It's about a mission to the sun. It's set somewhat in the future and the sun is losing its power. They send this huge bomb to reignite part of the sun. The bomb is the size of Vancouver or Toronto. It's immense. They built it in space, in orbit around the moon. It's called Icarus 2. There was an Icarus 1, which failed, and they don't know why it failed. Once it gets near the sun, they lose all radio contact with it. And they have to find out what's happened to them.

Psychologically it's about your relationship with the Creator, which in practical terms is the sun, but in spiritual terms you can widen it if you want to. It asks, "Can you meet your maker and survive?"

But we're also working on a book which hasn't been published yet. It's called *Never Let Me Go*, and it's by Kazuo Ishiguro. It's his new novel which will be published in March. It's brilliant.

Overstreet: You have a huge platform, but because of the tools you've used, you've inspired a lot of independent filmmakers. Is that an aim of yours, or just a happy development?

Boyle: I'm just better at making a film like that. I'm not as good at the big films. I've tried to make a big film, with *The Beach*. It wasn't a really happy experience. You sort of learn what you're better at. I love watching films on that scale, and when they're good, there's nothing better! You always have that remaining ambition to pull that off—the big one. When *Gladiator* unites the world, you're all watching *Gladiator*, you realize that cinema really is about a worldwide screen wrapping around the globe, watching these myths played out. But I'm not very good at it. You learn what you're better at.

But I do like to inspire people . . . particularly those without a voice, people who don't think they could be a filmmaker. I don't think it's a problem in America. People feel much more free in America. I think everybody thinks they could be a filmmaker. You've had ordinary kids like Steven Spielberg grow up to be the king. That's not true in Britain. It tends very much to be a fenced-off area, it tends to be the preserve of the intellectuals or the intellectual class, with only a few exceptions. It's a shame. So I do bang on about it in Britain.

Overstreet: You're such a creative, versatile artist. When you look at the top ten at the box office, does it discourage you to see such derivative, disposable work like *Boogeyman* or *Are We There Yet?* at number one when there are better films showing?

Boyle: Imagine what it's like if you work in a garage, or you work in a superstore, all week, and then Friday night comes along . . . and you've spent all week dealing with whatever you're dealing with, and you get one chance to take a girl or to go with your mates for a good laugh. That is part of our job. Entertainment.

The power of those people with their money will always make sure that the industry delivers to them certain kinds of entertainment. But you have to be very careful that we don't turn the movies into opera, which is like, "They're good for you, they're a bit specialized, and they'll be a bit beyond some of you." Within that, you've got to be, like Scorsese says, "cunning." You've got to smuggle good ideas into something that attracts that person to the Friday or Saturday night film. That way they get a bigger kick out of it than they do from those films you're talking about. That's the job. It's not like you've got to ban the bad films . . . you've just got to make better films more entertaining.

Overstreet: *28 Days Later* demonstrates what you're saying. In a way, it's just a big crazy zombie movie. But it an arresting relevance, and moments of powerful emotion.

Boyle: My favorite bit of *28 Days Later* is where the dad gets infected and he has to say goodbye to his daughter.

Overstreet: That's a heartbreaking scene.

Boyle: *Gladiator* does that too. It moves people. We are all moved, en masse. And we're moved by something common amongst us all.

Q&A with Danny Boyle, Director of *Millions*

John Suozzo/2005

From *Storyboard*, the newsletter for the Washington, DC Film Society website, March 2005. Reprinted with permission.

This Q&A took place at Landmark's E Street Cinema on March 7. DCFS Director Michael Kyrioglou moderated the discussion.

Michael Kyrioglou: Tell us a little bit about the film's development.
Danny Boyle: This script was written by Frank Cottrell Boyce who also wrote *24 Hour Party People* and *Hilary and Jackie*. He wrote this around four years ago and they took it round to a lot of other directors before they turned to me. They came to me last because I think they genuinely thought I would turn it into a child molestation zombie movie.
Kyrioglou: I understand that very little is left from the original script.
Boyle: The original script was set in the sixties. You may remember a wonderful black and white film called *Whistle Down the Wind* starring the late Alan Bates as a criminal in a barn. I thought our script was a little too close to that idea so we decided to change a scene here and there to make our film different from that one. And when all was said and done only one scene remained from the original script.
Q: Where did you find the young guy in the movie who played Damian? And could you tell me where you filmed the movie because I thought I recognized a few of the locations.
Boyle: We filmed the movie in Widnes, a town halfway between Liverpool and Manchester in the northwest of England. They're kind of twin towns really, though they hate to be referred to it as that because of the rivalries between the football teams. The little lad (Alexander Etel) was

new to films; I just caught him out of the corner of my eye. He wasn't the best actor of the people we auditioned but there was something about him that I couldn't pin down. The whole time I was thinking "It's him. I know it's him." And sure enough he was the person who became Damian.

Kyrioglou: There seem to be a lot of child actors in films recently, from *Finding Neverland* to *In America*. There seem to be a lot of very natural child actors today that are not like the annoying child actors who used to be too adult and too precocious to be believed. Also, can you discuss some of the scenarios we see in the film like the trains whizzing by and the housing going up?

Boyle: I grew up in Manchester and earlier films had portrayed it with a bleak industrial landscape. I always found it a bit like [Damian] sees it—a wonderful place. I wanted to emphasize the wit and vitality of the area. That's why we filmed in the summer even though the movie is set at Christmas time—I wanted to show off the blue skies and good weather of a Manchester summer. That was the only fallout I had with the kids. They said, "It was stupid" to wear coats and hats in the summertime. When I told them it was all to make Manchester look pretty they said, "It's still stupid."

Kyrioglou: I loved seeing bags of money all over the place.

Boyle: It's weird because in England it's a crime to burn real money. It's also a crime to burn fake money. So we can't admit to what we actually did during the filming. (Laughter)

Q: How do you have to adapt your directing style when you work with children?

Boyle: It's very interesting because you think you need to be highly interventionist at first. But if you start out like that, you kind of leave fingerprints all over them. So I backed off a lot and they gained confidence as a result. You tend to get a lot of praise if you do that, but it's the kids that deserve it because they are showing they understand what's going on. The best example of that is the scene when the boys look at bras on the Internet. If I told them what I think as a forty-year-old man about bras and the Internet it gets really complicated. I just let them play it as they wanted to. It was a really beautiful scene and they are responsible for it.

Q: I thought the film had a wonderful balance between fantasy and reality. How did you achieve that?

Boyle: There was one scene we had to cut with the saints, when they go up into the attic fleeing from what they thought was the bad man coming after them. All the saints gathered in the attic and started to pray. But they were so loud they gave themselves away to the robber so we had to cut the scene. I hoped that the house-building scene, with its point of view from inside the house, would tell the audience that I was telling this story from the child's standpoint.

Q: I was impressed by the look of the saints. Were all the saints' stories real?

Boyle: There's a patron saint of just about everything now. There's one for TV, Saint Clare, and one for the Internet, Saint Isadore of Seville. We have an aging Pontiff but other people within the Church are trying to keep up with the times. It's really kind of charming and they've had to double up the saints' duties. They're often the patron saints of four different things. Sadly, there is still no patron saint of directors.

Q: In the past, I thought your soundtracks were great, better than the one tonight. What happened?

Boyle: This soundtrack is more orchestral. I used John Murphy, who used to be in *Frankie Goes to Hollywood*, a very street-wise Liverpool kid. He did the music for *28 Days Later* and his role model was Danny Elfman who did *Edward Scissorhands*. I think in a kid's film that deals with magic you need a score, not a soundtrack.

Q: If this movie was originally set in the sixties, how did you work in the current plot element of converting Pounds to Euros that is so critical in the movie?

Boyle: Originally we were looking for an opportunity to show criminal activity. I had read a story about the unification of East and West Germany where they kept all the old East German currency under heavy guard due to the threat of criminal activity. We thought that if Britain decided to convert its currency, we'd have an incredibly topical film. But, alas, this is England, the conversion never happened and all we have now is a pure fantasy film.

Kyrioglou: Why'd you pick the old guy in the sleigh for the ad campaign?

Boyle: We actually talked to ad agencies to talk about what type of campaign you would need to run if the country actually did try to change their currency. They told us you wouldn't need to convince the young people to go along with it—it would be the older generation that would need convincing.

We chose Leslie Phillips, who appeared in the *Carry On* . . . films as a kind of risqué doctor, to appeal to the older people.

Q: Money seemed to be at the core of *Shallow Grave* and *Millions*. One ends well but the other ends poorly. Any reason for this?

Boyle: I think it shows the differences in England when each movie was made. The first movie was made in a cynical period when there was a Gordon Gekko, "greed is good" mentality prevalent. The second, made in the Tony Blair era, reflects the Labor Party trying to do good in the country. It felt like a different era in Britain.

Kyrioglou: What drew you to this project? We have grown to expect films from a dark place from you.

Boyle: I'm really a regular guy. I wanted to tell this story with vivacity. I don't want to look at the kids like they're victims. I wanted them to have the life energies . . . that Martha Stewart found in prison. (Laughter)

Q: I loved that the boy chose to bring clean water to the Third World, a worthy cause. Why did you choose that?

Boyle: I was simply looking for him to do a good deed. It turned out to be good that Damian is naive so he could address this problem from a child's perspective. It arose naturally out of the story. We actually found a company called Water Aid, a charity that we gave some money to, that builds wells in Africa. A bigger question is whether water should be a public utility or privatized. We felt it was urgent to highlight this problem.

Danny Boyle

Brendan MacDevette/2005

From *Independent Film Quarterly*, 2005. Reprinted with permission.

IFQ: *Millions* is quite a change for you, going from *Trainspotting* and *28 Days Later* to a story not only about children, but told with a great deal of innocence.

Danny Boyle: I know it looks like it is a drastic change, but it doesn't feel like it. When we were making it, it didn't feel all that different. The worry I have is that I'll make the same film again and again. And that fear becomes real from the inside of the process. From the outside, I can appreciate that it looks like a very different film compared to my past films.

I got the script and I just responded to it. A business decision would be, "Hey we made that movie, let's make another one because it was successful," or "Hey we made that movie, let's make something different." The decision was simply, I'm going to make that movie because there is something about it that I can relate to myself and makes me want to do it. It makes you want to spend a couple of years making it and publicizing it and makes you stand up for it, even if it gets slaughtered by critics, which they can do and you'll still be proud of it. You are disappointed if it's slaughtered, but you are still proud of it. I don't think you can do that necessarily which you've made for more of a business decision, and then they have to work. Then, you are living in expectation and not just hope. I always think that it is better to live in hope than expectation.

This film is made with an attempt to make money, but I have no idea if it will make money or not. It is not important in a way. I want it to be seen by as many people as possible because I am very proud of it. I admire people who can make the big movies, with all the big expectations on them. I love watching them; when they are good, they are really good. There is nothing better than a big movie. But I'm pretty sure, I'm not the right director for them. I like making up my mind on the day, making crazy decisions and you can't do that on big movies, there are too many people involved, there's too much money involved. I always say it's like an oil tanker, they are full of riches, but turning them around takes a whole afternoon to shift direction. I can't work like that; I have to be able to work like (snaps fingers).

IFQ: Did the religious elements of the film draw heavily from your Catholic upbringing?

DB: I made it because it felt like my background; I grew up a very devout, strict Catholic and was going to be a priest until I was about fourteen. All the iconography of the saints in *Millions* is very familiar to me. The writer, Frank Cottrell Boyce is a Catholic and remains a practicing Catholic. We spent a year writing the film together and even though it is a modem film, the ideas are very much rooted in our backgrounds. Certainly, the spiritual message of the film, if there is one, is based on something that we both share and believe. It is not a strictly religious sensibility, it has more to do with having faith in people and that goodness can come out of that. There is a sense of theatre in Catholicism. The drama and extreme stories that surround the religion and there are incredible Gothic tales about a lot of saints. They are quite violent, very dramatic and captivating, and that is the whole point of them, just like the movies, to captivate. That is the whole idea—to catch you in the headlights and captivate you.

IFQ: You have Saint Clare smoking a joint in the film. How did you want to portray the saints?

DB: We wanted the saints to have personality; we didn't want them to be pious or sacred or sanctimonious. We wanted them to be real people because they were and to the boy they are real people. They fizz with personality. Like Saint Peter, who is probably number two in the world, we cast him with a Newcastle accent, which is a town in the Northeast of England. That says something very emphatic about him, casting him as Newcastle. It is a very blue-collar, working-class town with a very defiant character. I don't know what the equivalent in America would be.

IFQ: Your first film *Shallow Grave* and now your latest *Millions*, although completely different films, both concern finding a bag of money. What is it about that situation that appeals to you and the responsibility that it commands?

DB: It's a great trick, in any movie, because a bag of money changes everything. It is like throwing a grenade into a room. It is a great starting point for a film. *Shallow Grave* came out of the milieu of the time. Margaret Thatcher was out of power, but her legacy was still there. So, it was very much like the film *Wall Street* and Gordon Gekko's "Greed Is Good" speech. *Shallow Grave* was very much informed by that cynical self-interest. Things have changed in Britain. Since 1997, we have had a labor government who has reintroduced the idea of community responsibility and that we have to build a social state, not just a place for individuals to flourish. They have poured money into schools and public transport. So the milieu today is very different and I wouldn't make *Shallow Grave* now because it wouldn't be appropriate. It wouldn't have that sense of modernity that I want all of my films to have. *Millions* shows that an act of generosity is possible in the modern age. I don't think you could have made this film at the time of *Shallow Grave* and feel they both very much belong to their time. Even though it is only ten years between them, which is nothing in terms of society, but they do feel like different societies.

IFQ: Do you think that the gesture the family makes at the end of the film to the African Village (£1000) is a large enough gesture compared to the shopping spree (over £200,000) they enjoy?

DB: I do think so because you can't be too idealistic about it. Damian doesn't get to spend all the money he would like to because it gets spent by other people and some of it gets burnt. He burns it because he is in despair that he'll never really get to spend it on what he wants. The bit of money that is left over at the end, he does get to win a small but important victory and put the money where he thinks it should go in Africa helping people get some water. Damian doesn't even think in terms of responsibility, the naiveté of his worldview that there is this money and it doesn't seem to make anyone very happy and just complicates things. On the other hand, there are these people in Africa who need the money.

IFQ: I'm interested in the responsibility of the father (James Nesbitt) who clearly chooses greed over the safety of his family; can you talk about that character's responsibility?

DB: That is what money does to people. Unfortunately, it changes them. When he first finds it, he says to the boys, we are going to hand it in. Then, he changes his mind and says he'll keep it and use it. There is that horrible scene, where he takes the money and shakes it out on the table. There is one moment where he snaps at the boys and says shut up and go to bed, and then he goes upstairs where he has that horrible scene with his son where he says, "We're on our own, there is no God, there is nothing, it is bleak and we'll just look after ourselves, shall we." And the little boy doesn't believe him; he fights for the way he sees it himself.

IFQ: So adult greed has not changed since *Shallow Grave*. They were vicious and mean-spirited in that movie.

DB: They were. I think money does that to us. Listen, one of the reasons we are so interested in bags of money is when we did *Shallow Grave*, we didn't have any money at all. In fact, we had to sell parts of the set, the furniture and stuff, to buy film to shoot the next part of the film. Since then, we've had money; we've had a bag of money thrown in our laps. When you have a successful film, they give you money.

IFQ: How do you feel about making a movie that says money is no good being distributed by a multibillion-dollar corporation (Fox)?

DB: (Laughs) This is funny because this building (NewsCorp building in midtown Manhattan) is so corporate and when I talked to them on the phone, I always pictured them being in some shambolic office in Manhattan. The entertainment industry is full of those contradictions. It has more to do with how you behave as an individual. I can't think to challenge the corporate nature of Fox. I wouldn't want anyone else distributing the film because they are brilliant at nurturing small films, like they did with *Sideways*, *Garden State*, and *Napoleon Dynamite*.

IFQ: What do you think will happen with the spirituality of the Damian character? As he gets older, will he become like his father?

DB: No, I don't think so. The idea is the older boy Anthony is his father. His father says, "Where did I get you?" like he is surprised, but actually they are the same thing. They are the same guy, in a way. I had the little boy Damian very much in my mind that he would become an artist. A writer, painter, or what I don't know, but his imagination is fervent and when he finds iconography outside of religion to feed it, he will develop it in different ways.

IFQ: Meeting the child actors, you can tell Alex (Damian) still has that innocence, while Lewis (Anthony) is thirteen and a little older and more cynical and you can tell there was some competition going on between them for attention.

DB: We treated them on set as complete equals down the line. But I explained to them when this process of publicizing the film started that chances are that only one of them would end up on the poster. That was a shock to their system and you could see them growing up in that moment. Marketing is really tough and I'm not in charge of it and I don't want to be in charge of marketing because I'm not very good at it. I try to always take pictures with the three of us, but they are always learning life lessons. You can't overprotect them because you have introduced them to this world and they have to make up their own minds about it.

IFQ: Is there a huge shift from the on-set atmosphere when you are directing a big star like Leonardo DiCaprio to working with unknowns?

DB: While filming *The Beach*, we were shooting a scene at night in Phuket in Thailand. It was a street scene and there were crowds on the street. I walked down the street with Leo and I don't know what it's like being him, but I got a little sense of it and it was incredible. You had thousands of people lining the street and I was walking back with the actors to the start of the shot and every single person was looking at him. I kept looking at them and not a single person's eyes looks at me. I was standing right beside him; all the eyes were just boring into him.

With the kids on the set for *Millions*, I kind of like being immature on the set and having kids on set is a good excuse. The crew thinks, oh he's behaving that way as part of the process for the kids, but I actually quite like behaving like that. You learn a lot, directing with kids. It is not true, that adage: you should never work with kids or animals. It's true that you should never work with animals. I've worked with animals and you should never work with animals, especially cats. But with kids, you learn a lot, you've got to keep your fingerprints off them, that's the key thing. You learn that very quickly because your instinct is that you think you are going to have to do all the work and guide them. You have to back off and let them play the scenes themselves. I would ruin it if I interfered too much.

IFQ: So, you are doing *Sunshine* next?

DB: Yes, which is a bit of a bigger budget. It's science fiction. It has a bigger budget than *Millions* and *28 Days Later*, but it's not huge. Sci-fi does cost more because you have to build everything. It is about a journey to the Sun. There is a mission from Earth to the Sun and they are taking a bomb to the Sun to re-ignite a section of the Sun that is failing. The bomb is huge; it's the size of Kansas. The real mystery of the story is that there was a mission seven years before and it's been lost. At the end of the movie, they do get to meet the source of all life in the universe. So, that's got to be worth ten dollars, isn't it?

Zombies, Smack Addicts, and Starbucks

Brian Libby/2005

Originally appeared at www.salon.com, March 2, 2005. Reprinted with permission.

British director Danny Boyle first burst onto the scene with the acclaimed Hitchcockian thriller *Shallow Grave* in 1994, and quickly followed it up with a bona fide pop culture phenomenon, *Trainspotting*. Then, Boyle promptly lost his way.

His next two films, *A Life Less Ordinary* and *The Beach*, boasted bigger stars (Cameron Diaz, Leonardo DiCaprio) and fizzled with critics and ticket buyers alike. When he countered with the biggest hit of his career, the thrilling and intelligent zombie picture *28 Days Later*, he had returned to an earlier formula of a lean budget, a cast of largely unknowns and an unapologetically grim story line.

That success has perhaps put Boyle, forty-eight, more at ease, and in control, of his career. His new film, *Millions* (opening wide March 11), is about two young suburban British boys who find a bag of money on the eve of Britain's conversion to the euro—meaning the money has to be spent right away. The plot might sound familiar, but Boyle turns it into a visually stunning film full of fantasy and dream sequences that question everything from material culture to the existence of God.

After a rough-and-tumble childhood in working-class Manchester, Boyle got his start in the theater, which gave him a knack with actors. But his greatest talent has always been on the visual side. There are so many images in Boyle's career that are branded on the brain: the squalid rock-club toilet in *Trainspotting* that becomes the unlikely setting for an Esther Williams-esque underwater dream sequence; the haunting view of an entirely empty London that begins *28 Days Later*.

Still, for all his talents, perhaps the best thing you can say about Boyle is that he's still just an unassuming lad. Directors doing press tours for their movies can get weary fast, but during a recent conversation, Boyle thanked me profusely for driving three hours to the interview, chatted boisterously about soccer (he explained to me why bullying Manchester United better represents the game than the "pretty" style of rival Arsenal), and talked as openly about his failures as his successes.

Q: Your films are very diverse, but to me there's a connection in how they collectively portray people looking for some kind of escape, whether it's heroin or society or zombies. Is that intentional?

A: There's a British poet called John Betjeman, who was the poet laureate. He used a term called "third way," way before Clinton and Blair. He said Britain used to be the idealized village society, and then later it became a more bleak industrial landscape. But the third way that's come upon us was High Street shopping, that commercialization and corporatization of the world where everything becomes the same—a Gap or Starbucks on every corner. I think all my films are about how much that third way of life today has a hold over us: how much you are dedicated to it, and also how much you want to flee from it.

Q: And in all your films the characters are faced with false idols to worship once they do escape, whether it's heroin in *Trainspotting* or a jungle utopia in *The Beach*, or a squeaky clean but more materialistic suburban environment in *Millions*.

A: When I was a kid my dad moved us to a better neighborhood just like they do in the film. I could feel him trying to get us out of the path that was set for us. My dad was a working-class laborer. He was a big man and worked all his life with his brawn, really. He worked in a power station at a stove boiler. But he was smart, and he knew enough to make sure that I didn't follow him. That's what gave my sisters and me the chance to break from the pattern that all my old school friends remain in. They're still in Manchester and they're doing not very interesting jobs, honestly. That's one of the reasons I made the film. My mom's dead now, but it was a kind of gesture of love to her and my dad.

Q: The *Millions* script reportedly was tinkered with for years. Was that a sign of trouble or just part of the process?

A: That isn't always a good thing, of course, but it was with this film. Frank Boyce [the screenwriter, who also wrote *24 Hour Party People*] and I worked together very well. Both of you have to give up a bit of ego. The writer has to take criticism, and as the director you also have to acknowledge that they are the writer, and their imagination created this thing. That relationship often gets spoiled by people wanting to be known as auteurs, who say that scripts are just the skeletal framework for the real film. But I don't believe any of that. This movie was Frank's idea. And then we bounced ideas off each other for a long time. I was also able to do that on *28 Days Later* with Alex Garland, and I think that's why it was successful. With *Millions*, Frank did a lot of drafts over the course of a year, and we completed it together. It was a very personal project for both of us.

Q: Working with child actors can be a real challenge. How did you handle it?

A: You have to be lucky. Child acting is not a profession that's well organized. The best people might never walk into the room on their own, and sometimes you have to do this endless searching. And when the filming starts, you can't let it be just a dreary sort of field trip where they're just led around. You have to involve them, and make the film feel like a playground for their imagination. It has to feel like the film belongs to them too. Any time I tried to really impose a strong direction with the kids, I'd go back and look at the footage and it was horrible. I was just watching kids say what they were told to say. You have to make it emerge from them, and if you can't do it, it's because it's wrong—not because they can't do it, but because it's not a genuine part of their world.

Q: And that worked?

A: Yes and no. The kids were interesting collaborators, because on one hand they're just sponges. Their brains are just waiting to soak up knowledge. I didn't have to tell them anything twice. But on the other hand it's tough working with kids because sometimes they're just gone, they're disengaged. You can threaten them, bribe them, all the things you do with actors when a scene's not working, and none of it will change things. You just have to close the set and go home for the day.

Q: How do you keep them from turning into the next child-actor tragedy later in life?

A: Film is a bit pernicious sometimes. It can flatter people and then drop them. I didn't want that happening to these kids. They're very vulnerable at this age to the glamour of the world. I remember at the Toronto Film Festival we had this hugely successful screening, and you'd see the kids getting a tiny glimpse of this vain world, and you've got a responsibility to protect them from things like that. There are obviously good things to be had in this life of movies, but it can be really cruel to you as well.

Q: What was it like before *28 Days Later*, when you were coming off perceived failure with *The Beach*?

A: I had a really tough time of it. I was wounded after *The Beach*. I'd really had enough of making a movie on that kind of scale. I went back to Manchester and made a couple of very small TV films with digital technology. And it was out of that, and the relationship I developed with the cameraman, that *28 Days Later* grew. The lesson to me was that you have to keep learning. You can't blindfold yourself and say, "No, I was right all the time and they're all wrong." You learn what you're good at and what you're not so good at, and how to harness the best of what you do.

Q: Are you a true convert to digital filmmaking then?

A: I love digital, but I think your story needs to have a reason to use it.

Q: You've also moved away from big stars like Ewan McGregor and Leonardo DiCaprio.

A: It wasn't so much them—they are both great guys—as the scale of making a film like *The Beach*. When you have that kind of money involved, all the departments have to know everything in advance. That doesn't suit me. What I'm good at, or at least I think I am, is making it up on the day. You set certain parameters with people, but the rest you're kind of doing it on the hoof. And that's a wonderful feeling, the energy you get from it.

Q: So what if *Millions* made a lot of money and you were offered another big-budget project?

A: Yeah [laughing], the little man on my right shoulder says, "Yeah, you shouldn't do it." But there's a little man on my other shoulder as well saying the opposite. Because I love big movies as well. There is something about film going all around the world showing on huge screens: It's an international language that we all celebrate together. You see a big movie like *Gladiator* and you want to make that. One voice is saying, "Do it! Do it!" And the other one is saying, "You'd fuck it up!" So it's a constant battle, really.

Q: And it's not as if your style is stripped down. Your movies have a lot of visual sophistication.

A: I always try to be ambitious, not in terms of budgets but in terms of being imaginative. I don't want to make documentary-type, socially realistic films I want them to be bigger than life. That's what the screen is about.

Q: What about your next film?

A: It's called *Sunshine*, and it's about the sun. It's written by Alex Garland. There's a mission called Icarus 2 that is taking a bomb to the sun to try and reignite a section of it. The bomb is the size of Vancouver and it's been built in space. There's been an earlier mission, Icarus 1, which has failed. And what's happened to it is a mystery. There's a religious element to the film—the sun is God, really.

Q: It sounds expensive—so much for not getting sucked into big-budget films, eh?

A: Well, we're trying to keep the price down, so it's nowhere near *The Beach* level. It's going to be somewhere between 20 and 25 million pounds (about $40 million). It also is probably going to have an ensemble cast without any really big stars. But it's hard to make it under budget because the dollar is so weak. There are all these bribes to go to Moscow or New Zealand or Toronto, because it's way cheaper, but we want to make the film in England and it's very expensive to do that right now.

Q: Ewan McGregor was unknown when he began working with you, and now he's Obi-Wan Kenobi—a real star. What are the chances of you working together again?

A: We fell out a bit over *The Beach* [McGregor was reportedly miffed that Boyle chose DiCaprio as his lead] but I've seen him a couple of times since then just to say hello. And there is a plan, a very long-term plan, to do a sequel to *Trainspotting.*

Q: You don't seem like the kind of director who'd make a sequel.

A: It's not an easy, cash-in sequel. It's to try and take those characters and look at them when they're about forty, when they're losing their hair and they've got all these decisions facing them about what they've done with their lives. But we don't want to shoot it until those guys really look like their best years are behind them. I think it will take another ten years still before they're sufficiently middle age. I want to look at these guys who've abused themselves so much and how they deal with the crisis of getting old.

Q: How did you get interested in film originally?

A: When I was a kid I used to go to this cinema in Manchester called the Aaben that showed these really weird films from Europe, partially because they had a lot of nudity, but also I loved the films—at least at the time. I've looked at some of them since and they're rubbish. But that's definitely where I got the bug. I couldn't get into the British film industry because it was very fenced off at the time, very clubby. And it still remains that way, I'm afraid. Our music industry on this little island has produced the most amazing bands, but our films are rubbish compared to music.

Q: Why is that?

A: Basically working-class kids join bands. You don't need money and you can just do it. The film industry isn't like that, but it needs to be. But it turned out well for me. I went into theater, because it was a lot more open. And theater gives you a lot of experience working with actors. A lot of film directors don't like actors. They think they're impenetrable and stupid. But I love actors, and I think that's become a strength for me.

Sunshine Superman

Amber Wilkinson/2007

From Eye for Film (eyeforfilm.co.uk), March 2007. Reprinted with permission.

You would think that after two weeks of solidly promoting his latest film *Sunshine* at screenings in London, Manchester, and on TV, radio, and in print, Danny Boyle would be getting just a little bit tired of the whole proceedings, especially since I am his penultimate interviewer on a day which began with a delayed flight from London to Edinburgh. Fortunately, he is unfazed.

"You can't think like that," he says, as he settles himself in the chair next to me in the bowels of Edinburgh's Scotsman Hotel.

In fact, the Manchester-born director—whose energy belies his fifty years—is more than happy to chat about his latest baby, a sci-fi block-buster set in space. With an ensemble cast including *28 Days Later* star Cillian Murphy, *Fantastic Four*'s flame boy Chris Evans, and Malaysian favorite Michelle Yeoh, it is set fifty years in the future. Global warming is a fear of the past, since the sun is now dying and the audience is strapped immediately into a mission with a handful of astronauts, who are in turn strapped to a bomb, which they aim to fire into the sun to kick-start its recovery.

Starting as a psychological thriller, then morphing into something much more akin to a creature feature, it has a similar claustrophobic feel to the first *Alien*. In fact, Danny was going to direct the fourth installment of the *Alien* franchise, *Resurrection*. But he admits that, at the time, he just wasn't up to the challenge.

"Funny isn't it," he says "I didn't know enough then. I really didn't know enough about filmmaking. There was this great script by Joss Whedon that was really interesting—more like the first film—very psychological and quite sexual in a way. I remember talking to Sigourney Weaver, and she said that's why she wanted to do it.

"Of course, the tensions came because the studio really wanted something like the second *Alien* film—an action movie, for the crew to chase the alien and be chased by the alien. And I thought, in that context I really don't know what you're doing, because that's going to be tough. I didn't know what I was doing and I wouldn't have known how to handle all the special effects that would have been a huge part of it. So I backed out of it. Thank God, I realized quite quickly."

Like the characters in his movie—who face difficult choices regarding their own destinies and that of the earth—control is important to Boyle. And it seems, the closer you get to Hollywood, the less say a director has. This may well be one of the reasons why he was happy to give up some budget in order to keep his hand firmly on the navigation controls.

"It's definitely a trade-off," he admits. "I think that when Alex (Garland) originally wrote the script for *Sunshine* he assumed that we'd have to go to Hollywood to make it because it would be an enormous budget, which sci-fi films tend to be, and I just didn't want to do that.

"I said we should do it like we did *28 Days Later*, in our place—this studio where we've worked before—and we should get Andrew (Macdonald) to control the film financially and then we can make all the decisions. We'll raise as much money as we can get and then just work within that field, all the time. It's a brilliant way to do it. Absolutely brilliant.

"That's the way you make a $40m film look like $150m, whereas if you take $150m, I guarantee $50m of it will be wasted; it will just dribble away through the cracks in the floorboards."

This might sound like a pretty extreme financial decision, but Danny is clearly a man who embraces risk.

"It is really nice to change, to do something different," he says. "I would never really want to do a sequel—I would find that really difficult to do, certainly not without a long gap, anyway. You want to approach it with a fresh set of guidelines or rules for yourself.

"This has been wonderful. When I look back at all the films I've done, suddenly I get a panic attack, thinking, how do you do this film? It is not just a challenge—that's such a bland idea—it's genuinely fearful, full of fear, thinking, 'I'm not going to be able to do this, am I?' And that's a good thing to have. Because when you are a director and you've had a couple of successes initially, people fawn round you and it's very—I don't know what the word is—it's very 'gout-ish,' sickly and kind of lazy and redundant. It is much better to think, 'I haven't got enough money,' 'How am I going to edit it?,' 'It's never going to be as good as . . .' That is a good place to be. I like that place."

There is certainly nothing lazy about *Sunshine*, which features breathtaking CGI visuals and creates a buttock-clenching tension throughout by carefully contrasting the enormity of space with the claustrophobia of the ship, the bright colors of the sun with the Icarus II's drab interior and sudden explosions of sound with the silence of the universe.

"Very good," he says when I bring this up, with an air of a teacher satisfied that his class has "got it." "Always try to accentuate extremes if you can. That's why *Trainspotting* is an extreme film. It could have been a more neutral film, a slightly more boring film. But we took a risk in making it extremely funny and extremely disturbing—and one bashes up against the next one. It's very risky, but I love doing that.

"I think people want that from cinema and we're going to need it more and more, because people don't just go to the cinema any more, there are so many other platforms they're going to watch through. So to make that cinema, that big event, it should be as much like a car crash as possible. Extremes of beauty and violence. And the sun is beautiful and violent—beyond imagination beautiful and violent—both those things, so the film should be full of that as well. That's what I always feel."

The concept of "beautiful violence" is certainly never far from Danny's work and can be traced back as far as *Shallow Grave* and *Trainspotting*. Despite his assertion that he's not keen on sequels, he is interested—at some point in the future—in directing Irvine Welsh's *Porno*, the follow up to the drug-addled *Trainspotting* set twenty years after the first novel. Despite not being asked about it, it is clearly at the top of Danny's mind.

"People want to know because they really love those characters," he insists. "John (Hodge) has done a bit of a version of it, to see if it works and it does work. They're older; they look older and that's the key. They have to look as if they creak a bit. What we didn't want to do was go back into it in the same place. We're waiting for the actors to age a wee bit, to put on a few years, really, I think it will be more interesting then. The characters will have aged and have a different perspective. And that hedonism that exemplified *Trainspotting*—that people love it for—that's gone."

But before that comes around, he's got plenty of other plans—and, as ever, he's taking things to extremes, set to encompass poverty and Pratchett. According to a recent interview, his next project is *Slumdog Millionaire*, based on the true story of an Indian who wins the local version of *Who Wants to Be a Millionaire*, only to be accused of cheating. More interestingly, perhaps, for those of us who loved his foray into kids' filmmaking, the vastly underrated *Millions*—which was shamefully forced to compete with *Revenge of the Sith* in its opening week—he is "working on another project with Frank Cottrell Boyce, based on Terry Pratchett's *Bromeliad Trilogy*."

The trilogy tells the story of a tiny race of people—Nomes—who live hidden among humans, and encompasses the books *Truckers, Diggers and Wings*.

"It's about seven years off," adds Danny. Fans will no doubt feel it is worth the wait.

Danny Boyle Talks about *Sunshine*

Ambrose Heron/2007

From FILMdetail.com, April 5, 2007. Reprinted with permission. Transcribed by Brent Dunham.

FD: Danny Boyle joins us. His new film is *Sunshine*, it's out this week. Just for people who haven't seen it yet, just give us the basic premise of *Sunshine*.

DB: So, in fifty years time, the Sun is dying and Earth is kind of frozen in a solar winter and there's this spaceship called Icarus II and it's got eight astronauts strapped to the back on an enormous bomb, a bomb the size of Manhattan Island. And they're attempting to pilot this bomb into the Sun and explode it there and, thereby, save our dying star. In order to get them to the surface of the Sun, they're hidden behind this enormous golden shield which has used all the world's resources of gold. Everyone's handed in their "bling" and it's all been melted down and it's an enormous enterprise. It's what happens to these eight astronauts as they draw closer and closer to the source of all life in our solar system.

FD: It'd be fair to say that this is more *Solaris* than *Star Trek*, wouldn't it?

DB: It certainly is. We always thought of it as more NASA than *Star Wars*. That was always the benchmark for it and it is a very intense experience, watching the film, which it should be really because you're actually pulling up close and personal to the Sun, our nearest star.

FD: When you make a film like this, I guess you got to bring up a bunch of scientists and say, "Look, we've got to get this, this and this right." Tell us a bit about the whole scientific research you did for the film in order to make it convincing.

DB: You do a lot of research with NASA and you base it on—they're working like twenty, thirty years ahead about what they're going to be doing. It's quite close to where we set the film, in a way, about what's going to be possible and what they'll do. For instance, to create oxygen on the journey, they have a fern garden and we have this enormous oxygen garden where all these plants are generating oxygen for the crew to use. So, it's real interesting, all that, and we got a science advisor, this professor, this physicist, Brian Cox, whose claim to fame, apart from being an extraordinarily brilliant man, is that he was one of the backing musicians in D'Ream and that was how he paid for his Ph.D. research. He was playing by night as a rock star and in the day doing the Einstein numbers.

FD: That is extraordinary.

DB: I know. It's a great story.

FD: If he was also the actor, Brian Cox, I'd be really impressed.

DB: Sadly, he hasn't quite done the acting number yet. But he did say to me the other day, "Oh, I could have played a part in the film, couldn't I?" So he's getting the bug for it. And he gave us a lot of advice about what is possible and what is impossible and you need something like that so when you want to leave it behind, you can leave it behind. Because the science is important to it, but it's the drama that's most important, the excitement of the film, the drive and energy, the journey. But he tells you when you need to leave the science behind.

FD: One thing that I was questioning in the film, because it's all done quite convincingly, would it be feasible to get a spaceship anywhere near the Sun? Would the Sun be so powerful it would just melt everything?

DB: Well, interestingly enough, the surface of the Sun is only 15,000 degrees Centigrade, which is an incredible temperature, but we do have a lot of satellites that go quite close to it. And that machinery, those instruments tend to operate in the same temperature range that humans operate. So, you could make a case for it being possible. Obviously, what happens at the end of this film is that Cillian Murphy, the scientist, puts his hand up and literally touches the Sun, which, obviously, people shouldn't try to do.

FD: If you get that near, yeah.

DB: Nor will you ever get a chance in your lifetime to do that. It is interesting how we've forgotten about it, really. All our ancestors worshipped it and we've kind of left it behind. The only reason we could come up with is electricity, that we've invented electricity which turns on the light. We sort of think we've got our own light now and we've sort of left it behind, the Sun. But if it blinks, we'll all be finished. Eight and a half minutes later, we'll all be wiped out, so it's quite important, yeah.

FD: Absolutely and one of the interesting things, not only is it a great plot device because it's crucial to life as we know it, but it's also kind of interesting, the whole spiritual dimension the film goes through. Because, like you said, it's been worshipped, it's been key to all life and certainly some characters on board have their own relationship with the Sun, don't they?

DB: Yeah, I mean the film starts off with this guy who has been sent on the mission to psychiatrically make sure they all stay sane. The first mission that's gone on has failed and they think the reason why is that everyone's gone mad probably, which actually turns out to be true, you find out much later but that's giving it away. So, this guy is like a psych officer but, of course, half way through the mission, he's as mesmerized by the Sun as anybody else. And he actually begins to see things in it which are beyond the rational, beyond the scientific, and that's the challenge for them, really: can they keep their sanity as they get closer to something which is beyond imagining, size and power-wise? When you begin to find out about it, doing the research, laying in bed at night, thinking about it, you can feel your brain pulsing, thinking "Oh my God. It burns millions of tons of mass every second. And, yet, it will burn for another four and a half billion years!" You just can't take on board something of that scale.

FD: Absolutely. The other thing you do, which is one of the real treats of the film is the visuals in order to convey the Sun. How do you create the Sun on film?

DB: Well, maybe this is the reason they've never made a film about it, because they couldn't capture it. I think its CG now. It's become so amazing now, its development over the last few years, what they can do now, and that's our image of the Sun as created by these CG artists. However, there is an old trick we use in the film, which is as old as cinema itself, which is when you're inside the ship, and the film is set entirely on the ship with these eight astronauts so it's this very intense, claustrophobic atmosphere. Everything is painted blue, gray, green. There's nothing orange or yellow or red. There's no strawberries or oranges, there's nothing in that color hue at all. So, basically, for twenty minutes, you get used to feeling a blue, gray, steel-blue world. And when they go outside, suddenly you flush the audience with this color palette that they've been denied and it's bit like a man dying of thirst and you suddenly drown him in cold water. It's like you've been penetrated by light and it's an old cinema trick: you hold something back and unleash it, hold something back and unleash it again. And that's one of the ways you do it.

FD: And, also, the cinematography, what you do is combine it really well, you've got all the claustrophobic stuff on the ship but all the Sun/space stuff. It's all integrated quite nicely, it doesn't feel like here's a CG bit and here's a live action bit. Was that part of the trick you were working with your cinematographer to create this sense of wholeness?

DB: That was what drove us mad trying to do that, to make sure that it didn't look like a CG movie, that it looked like you were on a real journey. This star, this thing we can't look at because it'll just burn our eyes, the movie gives you a chance to have a look at it, to stare at it. And to get lost in it, really, which is what happens to the characters as well. So it was crucial that it felt like as much a part of their lives as each other, you know? So, you didn't want it to be a separate element, it had to feel like it was the real thing, really. So that's why we set out with realism, with all the NASA research, is that you feel like you're on a realistic journey. And, hopefully, we fooled you by the end, so that you feel for a moment that you could stand and touch the Sun with your hand.

FD: What about the whole business of the different actors? Is it true you got them all living together in student digs in East London?

DB: It is, it is. At the University of Mile End in the student digs there by the canal, you can all go and have a look at it if you want.

FD: They're probably thinking the Dorchester, the Ritz.

DB: I think they all turned up thinking, "Is it the Dorchester or the Ritz?" And what you actually give them is Mile End University. And they were a bit shocked, I think, but it worked. Actors turn up on a film set and they have this bubble around them, a little bubble of self-awareness, of self-concern about their per diems and their overnights and their agents and their career moves. "When are the interviews?" and all this kind of stuff. And you've got to pop that bubble to make them part of your film so that it's unique and that's what we did. It's just like Alex Ferguson or Arsene Wenger or Jose Mourinho. You take a bunch of people and you create a siege mentality, you put them together and you say, "The world hates you, you do know that, don't you? It's just you alone, only you can battle this and fight through this." And it works, it binds them together. People that might not necessarily be the greatest of friends, they feel this bond. And that's what we did: for two weeks, we bombarded them with science and experience, they did flight simulators at Heathrow, they did scuba diving. All these kinds of different sensations you chuck at them to make them feel like this isn't any old film you're on, and it works. So that when you open the film, they've been together for sixteen months.

FD: In the studios, again in East London?

DB: Yeah, 3 Mill Studios which is shortly to become the Press Center. I believe you'll be there, for the Olympic Games. They're going to be converted into the world Press Center for the Olympic Games when they start in 2012.

FD: The scale of the film is so huge and yet you and your actors are in the studio in East London. Was it hard to imagine getting them into the whole business of what the film was visually?

DB: That's my job, really. That's your job as a director because what they're looking at is not what the audience are going to see. You have to somehow convince them, it's like you have to be a stand-up artist on a speaker's corner or something. You have to persuade them of what they cannot see yet, but what will be there. You become almost evangelical about it, trying to tell them what it is, and, if you get it right, hopefully their reaction is appropriate. And that's why, if you see the film and it doesn't look like CG, that's because you believe the actors, they're seeing something real. I think that's part of the trick of it, is to make sure that their reactions are appropriate to what they're seeing, to what the audience will eventually see.

FD: It's such a varied career you've had. I mean it's been about ten or eleven years since *Trainspotting*. That's such an iconic film in the nineties, did you ever feel pressured to do films like that or to make the step up and make more obviously commercial films? [*Trainspotting*] had such an impact, especially for my generation.

DB: Yeah, we've been very lucky with it, really. You get a lot of pressure but I've always tried to do stuff that interests me. You spend so long on each film and you sell it to so many people—to the people you originally pitch it to for the money, to the people who make the film with you, to persuade them to work late at night to work for you, to you guys now to promote the film and to let people know about the film—that it has to be something you believe in. I can't imagine what it would be like to make a film that you did for the wrong reasons. So, sometimes they feel commercial and sometimes they don't. But you treat them all equally, they're all equally important despite whatever their destiny is in the end. They're all equally valuable, I think.

FD: I mean certainly *Millions*, your last one, was a wonderful film even though it was smaller scale.

DB: A little film, you know? Not many people saw it, boo hoo—

FD: But there's still time. There's still time!

DB: Yeah, catch the DVD, obviously. You cherish them all, really. You often get asked, "What's your favorite film?" and you can't, it's like you've got three kids saying, "Who is your favorite kid, then?" You tend to look after the ones that have been ignored a bit, you kind of put an arm around them to look after them but, otherwise, they're all part and parcel of the whole thing.

FD: The guy I feel sorry for, after each film you do, is the guy who does the poster. We've got the poster for *Sunshine* sitting in the room here. The *Trainspotting* poster has got to be the most imitated image of our time. Spoofs, people just cut and paste it and use it and I always think the guy designing the poster for your new film is up against it, isn't he?

DB: To come up with something. It was amazing, that *Trainspotting* one. I remember Richard Branson was launching some Virgin thing and he copied it and we wrote to him and said, "Oi! This is our pozzie, you should be paying for this!" And he made a large donation to charity in lieu of some royalties or rights, so credit to him for that.

FD: With *Sunshine*, which is out in the U.K. this week, what kind of world-wide release is it getting? Is it coming out there soon or a bit after?

DB: It's launched everywhere in the world in April, at different times but all in April, apart from America where I think they're going to release it in either July or September; they're still trying to decide.

FD: It's an interesting cast because one of the ideas in the film—I guess China's become a super power so the leader of the team is actually a Japanese actor, but you've got Asian actors, American actors, British actors, kind of interesting cast, isn't it? And who they represent.

DB: It's very interesting because the realities of space travel are its staggering bill that comes at the end of it. They said in fifty years time, it's the Asian economies that will be paying for it and they'll probably be leading the technologies as well. So, you think it should be an Asian, or pan-Asian cast, which is what we tried to get. And an American cast because, obviously, that's the reality of making movies at the moment, but we tried to get actors from all over the world to play it. And it's real interesting, space, because they normally don't work in movies, kind of multinational casts. They always look a bit dodgy. You think, "Oh, the German actor's in it because there's a German bank involved" or stuff like that. So, we tried to get people from all over the world and bring them all together and there's no nationality in space, there are no nation issues in space. It kind of humbles and equalizes everyone, I think.

FD: Absolutely. Well, I hope it gets a good go because I definitely think it is worth seeing. And I think one of the good things about the film is that, even though it's not done on a $100 million budget, it got a nice scale to it. It does look like a proper movie the way you shot it, doesn't it?

DB: We wanted it to look like a $200 million movie, although we shot it for a lot less than that. Your money can go a long way if you work with it really carefully, and work with good people, and that's what we tried to do, really. It's certainly a lot better than a lot of the Hollywood rubbish you get tempted into.

FD: And what's after this? What's on the Danny Boyle pipeline?

DB: I hope to do a film set in Mumbai, in India. An amazing true story about a kid, a slum kid, who is uneducated, illiterate, and he goes on the Hindi version of *Who Wants to Be a Millionaire* and wins it. And the police can't believe that he can answer these questions that they don't even understand and they torture him to try and confess about how he's done it. When, in fact, the film shows how he happens to know the answers to the questions because of his life experiences. The real reason is a love story: a girl that he loves, he's lost in the chaos that is Mumbai, this massive, sprawling city of 80 million people. And all he knows is that she watches this show every night so he goes on there for all the right reasons and he wins it.

FD: We'll all look forward to that. In the meantime, *Sunshine* is out this week. Danny, thanks very much for joining us.

DB: Thank you very much.

Interview: Danny Boyle

Faisal Latif/2007

From Puremovies.co.uk, 2007. Reprinted with permission.

Danny Boyle has nailed nearly every genre in cinema and now, after turning down the opportunity to direct the fourth installment of *Alien*, he has opted to try his hand at science fiction. The cult director has already had an astonishing career, winning twenty-four awards along the way for films such as *Shallow Grave, Trainspotting,* and *28 Days Later.*

On a chilly Monday afternoon in London, Danny Boyle took time out of his busy schedule to talk to Pure Movies about sci-fi, romance, and his new film, *Sunshine.*

Q: So, Danny, was it your idea to make a science fiction movie or were you drawn into it by Alex Garland?

Danny Boyle: It was actually Alex's script that drew me into it, because he had this fantastic idea about eight astronauts strapped to the back of a bomb, and of course it was attached to an amazing notion about the sun. There's never been a film about the sun before, so it was an incredible experience to work on something like this, and you could actually feel your brain swelling with the enormity of such a premise. It was good to be able to feed that back to the actors to make their performances more efficient.

Q: It must have been hard to fill the footsteps of classic sci-fi films . . .

DB: We tried to follow the pattern of great sci-fi movies like *Alien* and *2001: A Space Odyssey* by filming in a narrow corridor. This was a weird sci-fi in its own right, but it boils down to basically a ship, a crew, and a signal. It was bizarre to work in such classic circumstances, but it was like creating an original movie at the same time because a film based around the sun has never been made before.

Q: Were you not linked to the fourth *Alien* movie at one point?

DB: I actually backed out of that because I was intimidated by the special effects, but doing a sci-fi was on the radar. And while I was making *Sunshine*, I'm sure it's true for a lot of directors, I realized I was a big fan of this genre. I always go to the premieres of sci-fi movies such as *Contact* and *Alien: Resurrection*, and I don't do that with other films so it was nice to be a part of this sort of film.

Q: How was the film received in America?

DB: It's funny because there's a part in the film where there's a little hope that shines through, and then we dash that almost immediately after introducing it, and that killed the Americans! They will do anything for hope, even if it means sacrificing all levels of plausibility, and they didn't like what we did there at all.

Q: Did making *Sunshine* perfect in terms of special effects prove expensive?

DB: It was filmed in the U.K. and was therefore cheaper than other films, but $45 million is a decent budget and we did manage to stick to it. We had more freedom because we didn't do it at Pinewood Studios; we decided to do it at the same place as *28 Days Later*, and therefore really made our money go further. The place we filmed it at was a lot smaller, but we got used to that, making it as real as possible for the actors as it would be inside the spacecraft.

Q: Is it true that you also made the actors stay in student accommodation in London for two weeks so that they could get the feel for what it would be like to be together for as long as their characters have in *Sunshine*?

DB: Yes, they had quite an experience with that, sharing toilets and sharing a kitchen. Apparently, they decided to cook fish one night and the dig smelled like that for two weeks.

Q: How did you create the CG?

DB: We used a company, MPC, who did the *Harry Potter* and *Narnia* films, and obviously their work is quite technical in terms of what they have to do when they create a dragon's tail, or a snake. This was a chance for them to do something totally artistic and a little different by creating a solar system that the audience could be sucked into, and instead of doing one small aspect of a creature they had total control over the whole project.

Q: How accurate are the scientific elements of the film?

DB: Well, we brought in Dr. Brian Cox to check over the script and remove anything that was wrong, but Alex's script was written quite accurately and by reading it you can tell he's a big fan of sci-fi and knows what he's talking about. But the fact that the sun is going to die is true, and that aspect of the science is definitely sound. Even though it will happen in a very long time, that important fact is that it will happen.

Q: If it was going to happen next year, how would you spend your last year on earth?

DB: I've recently returned from a visit to the Taj Mahal in India that I've never been to before, and it was the most beautiful and romantic place I've ever seen, and I'm not really a romantic guy. So I'd go back there, and I'd urge others to do something as equally romantic.

Q: What did you learn about yourself after making this movie?

DB: That I never want to do another sci-fi! You'll often find that unless they have a contractual obligation, directors tend not to go back into space, and I think that's because the standard set by classics is so high that you have to get to that point reached by them, and its fucking exhausting doing that, especially as you've got to do it at every point throughout the film, and what's more you've got to push everyone else to that standard.

Q: What conventions or standards did you feel you had stick to? Did you abide by any specific rules previously created by the classic sci-fis?

DB: Well, we tried a romance but realized that it didn't work because it hadn't been done before. *2010: The Year We Made Contact* tried to do it, but even there it didn't take off, so we decided to leave it out. Renoir once said that on set you should always leave the door open for life to walk in, and a convention of science-fiction films made in space is that you can't leave that door open, and you have to have everything in order before you set out on the journey.

Q: You have worked with Alex Garland before when you brought *The Beach* to the screen, and with Irvine Welsh on *Trainspotting*. Have you any plans to make any other novels into movies?

My favorite one is actually already being done. It's a novel called *Blindness*, and it involves an all-blind cast, so exactly how you go about doing that is going to be quite interesting to see.

Q: What is next for you then?

DB: I'm going to be filming in Mumbai for *Slumdog Millionaire*, a script written by Simon Beaufoy [*The Full Monty*], and the casting is currently the problem because it involves two Indian brothers and a sister, at ages eight, twelve, and sixteen, so that's what'll be keeping me busy for a while!

Peter Hawley Interviews Danny Boyle

Peter Hawley/2007

Interview conducted July 17, 2007, and posted December 1, 2007, on flashpointacad emy.com. Reprinted with permission of Peter Hawley, Chair of the Film and Broadcast Department at Flashpoint, The Academy of Media Arts and Sciences. Transcribed by Brent Dunham.

PH: Hi, I'm Peter Hawley from Flashpoint Academy, from the Film Department there. We're with Danny Boyle who is in town for *Sunshine*. We saw it last night. We took some students and we loved the film. I think the whole audience loved the film and thank you for taking the time to talk to us.

DB: It's a pleasure. Thank you.

PH: What do you think it is about science fiction, and space films in particular, that is attractive to directors? All the great ones, and you, too, have done it. What do you think is so attractive?

DB: I think it's like mountains or the Wild West used to be. Like mountaineering movies or the Wild West, it's a frontier that you pit yourself against. And it's interesting, as we conquer, literally, more and more of the planet, we will look to space more and more as a wilderness. It's a way that you can look at yourselves. It's a way Man looks at himself. It's a weird thing to do: to go out there in a steel tube because no sensible animal would do it. Because it's hostile, everything. If there's any weakness in that steel tube, you're all dead because everything is designed to kill you, everything. And, yet, we go there. And not only to do we go there, we send our finest scientists up there. We train them, our precious things, our finest people, and we send them up there to try and discover what's out there. And it's a way of measuring your own self and it's a way of, obviously, finding other consciousnesses. Are there other things beyond our little rational world that we imagine is so important?

PH: Well, it's great because, as a filmmaker, you get to invent that world, especially the Sun. How do we handle that suspension of disbelief? I mean, we sat there as an audience and said, "Oh sure, they're going to the Sun. No problem." And we buy into it on the first shot.

DB: Your basis is realism. Everything I try to do, I try to base in realism. But you don't stay realistic. And, at the end of the film, the guy puts his hand up and touches the Sun. I mean, it's just completely ridiculous in one sense but because you're grounded in a kind of realism and you make realistic images in the beginning. So, you see them growing their own food and cooking it, so it feels tangible and real. It's not like fantasy, you've set it into a realistic bedrock and people begin to go along with that, they begin to go on the journey with you. And the premise of the film is that you trap the audience in the ship. It's not like there's alternative scenarios you can go to, different planets or things. You're in this ship and everything you feel and experience is like they do as well. It's almost like you're in real time with them eventually.

PH: You mentioned something last night, which I really agree with, that we never cut back to Earth, it didn't become a disaster movie. It became this journey. Talk about that a little bit. Was there ever a version of the script where you cut back to Mission Control?

DB: No, there were a few attempts by the studio to put that ingredient in because I think it makes it seem safer to them. The premise was always like *Alien*, the first *Alien* film, which is you just find yourself in this ship. And when they leave the ship, you leave with them, but when they don't, you just stay there with them. And you feel like you're embedded in the mission with them. That was always the premise of the film.

PH: Can you talk about the casting a little bit? Unlike a lot of big, Hollywood films there's not the one star you hang your hat on, George Clooney or whatever. George Clooney's wonderful but talk about the casting and your approach to casting.

DB: Again, space is really interesting because it suits ensemble casts, where you have a group of equals and you don't quite know what their status is going to be. There's something about it. It's so powerful, so awesome, that it equalizes everyone and it's got huge advantages, of course, because then you can kill them off in any order that you want as a filmmaker, which is a great advantage. But you shouldn't really know who is going to emerge out of it as the one who lives the longest or the one who delivers the mission. It's actually Cillian in the end but it could be anybody in a way.

PH: At Flashpoint, we talk about collaboration a lot and I think a lot of young filmmakers think they have to have all the answers, they have to know how to do everything and they try to do everything, but in a film like *Sunshine*, and your other films, too, you have to branch out. You're starting with a screenplay, certainly the special effects. Talk to us about how you work with other people and other departments, special effects in particular.

DB: One of the skills, really, that you have to learn early on is how dependent you are on other people's skills, and it's finding a way through that. And you mustn't get scared that your vision is going to be lost in them. There is a danger, there are circumstances where that can happen but usually what those people are there for is to make your vision better, to improve it, really. In fact, one of the problems with success is that people start to drop their contribution and think you're a genius and you do it all yourself. You don't. You're really dependent on the contribution of others. And we always try to create a kind of family atmosphere and I think of my chief collaborators, like the cameraman and the designer, the costume designer, the script writer, you think of them like mini-directors, that's how I like to think of them. They're like little mini versions of me, really, and, ultimately, you have the responsibility to pull it all together. But that's what you're trying to find from people is ways of improving stuff, making it better. There are things that you feel fanatical about, that you know you're not going to change, no matter what people say. But you have to be aware of that because people will, like water, try to find the easiest route and sometimes that's not the most interesting route. And you have to know when to protect your vision and say, "No, I'm adamant. I'm going to do it like this," and you stick to what you want.

PH: I would think, just with all the history of great space films, *2001* and others, too, when you went to sound design it would have been daunting. You've got a voice of a computer, you've got all the silence of space and you have all the great sounds of the heat shield and the Sun and everything else. Talk about the sound design.

DB: I mean, [with] any movie, sound—despite the fact that they're treated on the set as the lowest of the low—everybody's going, "Oh, Sound wants to do that again? Why do we have to do that again?"

Sound is 70 percent of a movie. If you run movies without sound, or you do the sound poorly, they just don't work. They will not work. We've always tried to protect the amount of money we invest on sound to give them a rightful status, really, especially in a space movie because there's no sound in space. So, that's a challenge to you, straight away: there's no sound here, what are you going to provide for people back on Earth to watch the film? And, obviously, the biggest example of it is *2001* which took it to a new level of both—technically to a new level but also imaginatively. It was so bold, the use of classical music. So, you've got this challenge to you, really, and what we tried to do is use this group, Underworld, who I've worked with a number of times on *Trainspotting*, *The Beach*, and stuff like that. I wanted them to do a score but I didn't want them to be inhibited by the fact that it was their first score. I didn't want them to get all serious about worrying about climaxes, I just wanted them to experiment with the film. And they did that, and then I got my more conventional composer, John Murphy, to manipulate that work and add his own themes to it so that you kind of deliver a traditional score but it's experimental as well.

PH: As we're wrapping up here, I want to talk about film students and film schools. Everyone has a different path how to get there and, first off, you know you're a hero to film students everywhere. Students talk about *Trainspotting* and then they talk about *28 Days Later* and, many times, they don't realize that the same person made it, so you are a hero to film students. Can you tell us briefly your path to get here? I know it's different for everybody but I know our kids, our students, will be really interested.

DB: Well, I loved films but I couldn't see how to get into the film industry. This was in the eighties in Britain, it was a closed shop, you couldn't get in. I wrote to all the people and they didn't write back, and they never do write back. You just got to make your own way, really. The key thing to remember is that it isn't a door that lets you in because, if it was, there'd be a huge queue of people and the rich would be in the front and the poor would be at the back. There isn't a way. All there is, is obsession, really, and there is a natural wastage that gets rid of those people who are too romantic about it. But if you're mad about it and obsessed enough, you'll get there eventually. The industry needs your energy, that obsession you have, which usually comes with youth and it's slightly mad and deranged and pitiful and all those kinds of things. That's what it feeds off. You won't feel it at the moment as students but we need you to refresh the industry. We're desperate for you, so keep at it. I eventually went into the theatre. I started in the theatre because it's a lot easier to get in to and it is a good training, nothing to do with visuals, but it's a very good training because you become accustomed to working with actors. You're very comfortable with actors and a lot of film directors either fear them or loathe them, but, actually, they are your way out of every corner you paint yourself into. So, I did it that way and then eventually I got into television, I started doing a few dramas for television and then I picked up a script, *Shallow Grave*, and that's where I got started.

PH: And it's terrific. Well, thank you very much and next time you're in Chicago maybe you'll come to campus and talk to the students?

DB: Sure.

2007's Space Odyssey: Q&A with *Sunshine* Director Danny Boyle

Kevin Polowy/2007

From AOL/Moviefone.com, July 2007. Reprinted with permission.

Director Danny Boyle seems to live for dabbling in different genres—and bending them all—each new film markedly unlike his last. He's moved from dark dramedy to romantic comedy to horror to family with stops everywhere in between. Now the much-admired filmmaker behind *Trainspotting* and *28 Days Later* has left Earth and all of its limitations behind for the far reaches of sci-fi with *Sunshine*, a clever and creepy space thriller in which a team of scientists prove humanity's last hope as they attempt to reignite a dying sun. The film reunites Boyle with his *28 Days Later* screenwriter Alex Garland and star Cillian Murphy, and also features impressive turns from Chris Evans, Rose Byrne, and Michelle Yeoh. Boyle sat down with Moviefone to talk about the challenges of sci-fi, the status of the *Trainspotting* sequel *Porno* and how he responds to fans arguing over the merits of his filmography.

Q: Is there any genre that you wouldn't work in?
A: Space movies. [Laughs] Never again. It is interesting that directors usually only do one, unless they're a franchise and they have to do *Part II*, *Part III*, whatever. They only ever do one. Except James Cameron he's about to go back to space with *Avatar*. But he's a nutter anyway so . . . The rest of us people, you ever only do one, it's just really tough.
Q: Because no one hears you scream in space?
A: [Laughs] I don't know what it is . . . Actually I do know what it is because I've just done it. The demands of getting to that level that's been set by all those predecessor films is really tough, and you don't realize how tough it is until you start trying to do that stuff: weightlessness,

the isolation, lack of anything to cut to, there is no other scene you can cut to, unless you do a disaster movie where you can keep cutting back to Earth. So that was really interesting. I mean I'd love to do a musical, that's what I'd love to do. Because I think even probably more than space movies, that is the Holy Grail if you can make it, because to make a believable modern-day original musical would be very, very tough.

Q: Are we talking about something like *Hairspray* or *Chicago*?

A: Not a theater musical, because they all have an excuse for the singing. Either the scenario's familiar or there are the songs that everybody knows already. But I mean with original music and a modern-day setting. Not set in the theater or in the past. It would be so tough.

Q: It'd be a modern-day musical infused with that Danny Boyle brand of electronic music?

A: Well yeah, you think, what is modern music? And it's Rhianna, it's not Cole Porter. It's Rhianna or it's Justin Timberlake or whatever. So I guess it would have to be influenced by that somehow.

Q: You talk about some of the challenges to making a sci-fi movie, what are the advantages? Can you get away with more in the narrative or with the jargon? Play up the fiction part of the science fiction?

A: There's a hokey vocabulary kind of thing that you can talk about. Things depressurizing and whatnot. That's quite interesting. I don't know whether it gives you latitude. I mean, on the plus side you do get to create a complete world. You do get to make the rules of the world. And there's nothing to challenge that, because you set them and you make those rules so that everything has to follow those rules. But the downside is that it's very claustrophobic, because once you see all the s*** and the rules, once you start the journey, that's it. You can't then just bring something into it that isn't part of that world. It's very difficult to, anyway.

Q: You've had a few actors really jumpstart their careers in your films, folks like Ewan McGregor, Cillian Murphy, and Naomie Harris. Is there anyone from *Sunshine* that you see following that trend?

A: They're not discoveries, really. They're more people who have a track record or people that I always wanted to work with or I've admired, like Cliff Curtis and Michelle Yeoh, people like that. You think that you have to get them in a film one day, but more than likely you'll never get them in films, especially one in which you can put them all together. That's what great about space is that you can use an international cast and it's not a big issue. Nationality doesn't matter, race doesn't matter.

It's quite difficult to think of scenarios on Earth where you can do that; casting tends to be quite self-conscious. In space you just accept it; you just go "OK, that's the crew."

Q: Were there any particular roles that you'd seen these people in that made you think, "This is the person that I want for this role"?

A: I tend to watch actors and just really like them. Michelle Yeoh, always loved her, saw her in the Bond film and then *Crouching Tiger*, and always thought, "God I'd love to work with that woman." She's so independent and so her own woman. So we met her first, actually, and offered her anything, because again the roles are not gender-specific. You could cast them male or female, well, most of them. And then Chris Evans, I just met in a room. I hadn't seen *Fantastic Four* yet, it hadn't come out. But I met him in the room and we just thought he was a wonderful actor. So I didn't have any preconception of him. I think a lot of people have a preconception about Chris because of *Fantastic Four*, but I didn't have that. I just thought, "This is an excellent actor." I come from the theater, originally. I feel like Chris could go on and do Iago in *Othello*, he could just walk on stage and do it. Whereas lots of actors you work with in films can't. But he's a proper actor, he knows how to do it. And Cliff Curtis, I had seen him in *Whale Rider* and *Training Day*. He was excellent in that. Troy Garity, I'd never seen in anything. I watched *Barbershop* after I cast him and I didn't really recognize him anyway. He's excellent. The casting director said, I think you should see this guy, he's very underrated, very special, so I just cast him.

Q: He has the pedigree, obviously [as son of Jane Fonda]. He's making it. I mean he played "Intern" in *Conspiracy Theory*.

A: He's making his own way. I don't think he ever mentioned once, you know, where he comes from and all that stuff, because he really wants to do it himself. So he was excellent.

Q: At what point did you, [screenwriter] Alex Garland, and Cillian Murphy decide to work together? Was it a group decision or did it just come together piece by piece?

A: Well, we started casting the film and we hadn't thought of Cillian initially. I think that's probably because we saw that [his character] would be American and we know Cillian more from British movies rather than things like *Red Eye* or *Batman Begins*. But then I think we had seen *Batman* and thought that he was superb. He nearly steals the film and his American accent is impeccable. It's weird, the Irish are really good at American accents. So we thought, why not Cillian, and we read him like we read everybody. And he was fantastic, so he earned the part. And then we thought, this makes such sense, because the success of *28 Days Later* is what allowed us to have [a $40 million budget]. So we can cast whoever we want up to that level and then it suddenly made a lot of sense to have Cillian in it again. So yeah, sometimes the most obvious thing has to pop up in front of you.

Q: Had you guys ever contemplated doing *28 Weeks Later* together?

A: We talked about it, and there was always a possibility of doing it. But [*Sunshine*] took so long, that I couldn't contemplate it at all. And I know that although he is uncredited, Alex did write some of the script. So we made a mark upon it really, and I kind of recommended [director Juan Carlos Fresnadillo], and I also recommended the designer and the editor and the composer. It bears strong connections with [*28 Days Later*], but I think it was very useful to let someone else do it, to get a different eye on it.

Q: What did you think of *28 Weeks Later*, once you saw the final product?

A: I thought it was good. I was quite surprised when I saw it. I'll tell you, I was surprised and shocked to see how violent it was. I was completely shocked and thought, wow, was the first one this violent? You don't feel it yourself because you're involved in making it every day. But when you watch something fresh, it was like, f***ing A! I think I said to them at one point, "Don't you think you should tone down some of the violence?" And they looked at me like, what are you talking about? They were like, "You made the first one and that was so violent." But yeah I enjoyed it. I particularly thought that the opening forty minutes of it was just excellent.

Q: Your fans are constantly clamoring about a sequel to *Trainspotting*. Do you think *Porno* will ever make it to the big screen?

A: Well we've done a script, based very loosely around the book. John Hodge, who did the original script for the first one, has done a pass on it and it works. It's just a quick draft to see if the basic setting works, and it does work. And it's basically around Begbie, who's been in prison for twenty years for manslaughter, so that's the age difference. They were in their early-to-mid-twenties [in *Trainspotting*] and they're now middle-aged. And it's all the same actors playing all the same characters, and they are forced back together again by Begbie, and we will see what happens to them. What's good about it is the headiness, these guys who've done the absolute limit with themselves, are now middle-aged and you can't do that anymore. Time has taken its toll, and that's what we're committed to as an idea. Now the problem with the actors is that they don't look particularly different, they maybe look a few years older, but not much And actors do stay in that stage for a long time where they look basically the same, unless their hair falls out or something. They still look like they could play late twenties. But we want it to feel like a generation has passed by, like if one of them had a kid, the kid would be the same age as they were when the first film was done. And if it works, when they are that old and if they do indeed look their age it will be interesting because not only will the characters have a history, which we'll make, [the actors] have a history. So it'll have a resonance, I think. And the audience will be made of people who watched the film when it first came out who are now middle-aged themselves or new fans who like the original film. So I think it's a great idea. We just have to be patient with everything and wait, really.

Q: There seems to be a lot of debate around your films, particularly among your fans that have their clear-cut favorites and then that one film they don't care about as much. Take movies like *The Beach* and *A Life Less Ordinary*, films people have wildly different views on. Do you ever engage in those sort of debates, or try to avoid them?

A: It's funny. I mean the ones that people really like, like *Trainspotting* and *28 Days Later*, they sort of take over. People tend to know more about the movie than you remember yourself. So you tend to sort of let [those movies] go a bit and in a way become slightly a stranger to them. The ones that you have to protect are the ones that people didn't like as much [laughs]. So you tend to be a bit more protective of those ones that didn't do as well for whatever reason. Listen, I can't tell you what it's like but one day you think you'll never ever make a film and suddenly you've made half a dozen and people have an opinion on them. I'm lucky, really, to have made a few. When I made the first film [*Shallow Grave*], there were a group of people around making films and some of them never got to make another film. So I'm quite lucky to be in that position. And listen, not all of them are going to be quite popular, you quickly learn that. But it doesn't make them necessarily worth less. Although I think there are reasons that certain ones are more popular than others.

Q: But even the less popular ones have their fans that will staunchly protect it.

A: I think there are bits in them that are brilliant. I mean there are bits in *A Life Less Ordinary* that are absolutely dazzling, I think there is a dance sequence in it that is just wonderful and they are really good together, Ewan McGregor and Cameron Diaz. So I don't know, it's interesting.

Q: I look forward to the musical.

A: [Laughs] I don't think it will be next.

Boyle's Orders

Hank Sartin/2008

From *Time Out Chicago*, November 13–19, 2008, issue 194. Reprinted with permission.

As part of the Chicago International Film Festival, director Danny Boyle—the man behind *Shallow Grave, Trainspotting, A Life Less Ordinary, The Beach, Millions, 28 Days Later,* and *Sunshine*—brought his new film, *Slumdog Millionaire,* to town. It's an almost epic tale of a boy who survives the slums of Mumbai and becomes a winner on the Indian edition of *Who Wants to Be a Millionaire* while tirelessly pursuing the one woman he loves. We spoke to Boyle, who is almost alarmingly enthusiastic and loquacious even at 8:30 a.m., in a hotel suite that made for an interesting contrast with his mostly slum-set film.

TOC: I told a friend of mine I was interviewing Danny Boyle, and he said, "Which Danny Boyle is that? The *28 Days Later* Danny Boyle or the *Millions* Danny Boyle or the *Sunshine* Danny Boyle?" Is that just about scale of production?

Danny Boyle: Yeah, except the only one that's really properly scale is *The Beach* because that's the only film I've done that's had a proper budget, you know, that's had a serious budget. Everything else, we've tried to, we've really tried to make look big sometimes. But with a film like *Millions,* it would be inappropriate if it looked big because it feels like a more . . . But *Millions* cost the same amount of money as *28 Days Later,* which is regarded as a much bigger film, so it depends what you do with the results, I suppose. One thing I know for sure is that I've decided sort of that—as soon as I say this, I'll change my mind, of course, as soon as the interview's over—I've decided not to do those big-budget films. I don't think I'm very good at them. I much prefer to make, to have a slightly more limited resources. You do get free, as everybody knows, you do get freedom of expression more like that. You have less people trying to work the film with you when you spend less money. Obviously you don't have the equipment, blah, blah, all that kind of stuff, but those are sacrifices that you make. And I've sort of decided like that in terms of material, I don't feel as much of a difference between things as other people recognize, obviously, in terms of their impacts. And I tend not to think about it as well, you tend to just focus really, you don't really think about the connections between the films. You just concentrate, well, I don't anyway, I concentrate on the narrative and the characters and the ideas and one thing at a time. And if things connect—and I've got to be honest, some days, you're doing something and you think, "Ah! This is exactly the same . . ."

TOC: "That thing from before . . . !"

Boyle: Yeah, yeah! The self-consciousness is a major enemy, I think. I don't find self-consciousness really useful at all, so you tend to do these interviews where you are made aware of it, and thankfully an amnesiac drug is released in you when you go back to work, and you tend to forget all these things. I don't know what it is, because now you remember them, but they fade, and you just get on with the film and the story.

TOC: I'm going to ask one more connection question, and then I promise we'll stop and just talk about *Slumdog*. This is the third film you've made that's involved a huge sum of money that I'm going to argue isn't really about the money. Is that, but on the other hand, one you start intensely dark, the money corrupts and shallow grave and all these people are at each other's throats, basically. And then *Millions*, which says money can be a dangerous, corrupting thing, but the eyes of a child sort of saves it. And here we've got money, it's like, hooray! Money! Twenty million rupees! This is fabulous!

Boyle: He's not really after the money, and that's why he wins it, actually. In reality, it's a very, very difficult show to win in India, because supposedly what happened is that when the show began, a lot of very clever people disguised themselves as rickshaw drivers, as poor people, and they started getting some very high-water cash. So what they did is that they made the questions much more difficult, and it's a much more difficult show than America or the U.K., the level of questions. It's also lots of cultural things that you couldn't answer, but there's certain things you think, "Fuck! That question!" Twenty, thirty rupees for like $2,000. You think, "What? I'd never get that question!" So they've made it very difficult, like that, so it's a very difficult show to win. So he would never win the show anyway, even if he didn't have all these useful connections, because in fact he makes two or three guesses which are not based on his previous experience—or directly anyway. The reason he wins it is an Indian thing: He is relaxed. His agenda has nothing to do with the money. He doesn't have that thing you see on the real show where people go "Oh I don't know this, but if I don't get this question right I'm sure I'll get the next one." The escalator beckons, and he never thinks like that. All he wants to do is stay on as long as possible. That's his agenda, in the hope that she will see him.

TOC: One of the things I was immediately struck by in *Slumdog Millionaire* is that this is kind of an old-fashioned romantic story.

Boyle: Timeless.

TOC: Yeah.

Boyle: We call it old-fashioned but it's actually timeless; I think something still stays in our hearts about dedication and loyalty and the way that he stays loyal to her and he just will not let her go. At each age [we see him], she's ripped away from him by circumstances, torn away from him. But he always stays loyal to her. They stay in each other's hearts.

TOC: The word Dickensian comes up in writing about the film, which makes perfect sense. It's the girl who's right for him, it's *Great Expectations*, but then you get a little *Oliver Twist* thrown in.

Boyle: Very Dickensian. I remember talking earlier to Simon about it and he obviously mentioned it. He is aware of it. It's true. It's the extremes of storytelling that are available in India now. We don't have quite as much now in the West because we've now built comfort zones around our lives. You don't get that in India, it's still extreme. You still get this sense that Dickens had of this incredible city emerging, burgeoning itself forward, changing every day. And within it, incredible opportunity for wealth and riches being generated instantly, and then this massive population of people—especially in East London—living in poverty and unbearable conditions.

So you'd have these same massive extremes and the corrupt police force in India. For storytellers, it's melodrama, it's fantastic, and it's real at the same time. As opposed to the West where we pop the melodrama into fantasy films now and it's what we've done for the past fifteen years: *The Lord of the Rings* and *Batman*. It's become the default setting, fantasy. We don't challenge it or don't sense it is a genre anymore. There's going to be two or three superhero films next year, we just know it. They'll be the top films of the year and I'm sure it's because of that we can't work the extremes of drama into our realistic films anymore.

It's very difficult; people just won't accept it as much. They just think it's . . . melodrama rather than realism.

TOC: Do you think that's a change—this is asking for cultural punditry but what the hell—that we've gotten used to these conventions in film or is that a change in the way we interact with . . . you were talking about the extremes in society, right? I look around; here we are in Chicago where there are incredible extremes of poverty and wealth, this hotel suite itself . . . let's not think about what they actually charge for it. We're in the part of the city where people pay $2 million for a condominium but down on the street to get here I walked by at least half a dozen homeless people. On the other hand, that's a little different than Dickensian London. Is it that the life has changed or is it that we can't accept that in movies anymore?

Boyle: I just don't think . . . we just don't seem to accept it in movies anymore I think. I think it's because there are safeguards that we— that's what I meant by the comfort zone, for our own morale. There is a procedure through which the poor can go or be helped to go through. Whereas in India it is like Dickensian London; it's every man for himself. None of those structures have been built yet; they don't even have proper water facilities for the slums, or proper sanitization. So there is not going to be any health and safety regulations. They'll take a long time to clean up the water and sanitization, so there isn't that provision to help people on certain levels. It is just every man for himself. Except of course self-support comes in because of the slums. They don't have any state support so they rely on themselves. There are extraordinary neighborhoods that are very resourceful and very protective of their own and they look after each other as a community. They are self-perpetuating of course because people within that community know "Fuck, I don't want to go on living in one of those cancer flats they're offering me outside of the city because I'll have nothing, man. I'll still be poor. I'll have bricks and mortars, but I won't have the sense of millions of us protecting each other." It's fascinating like that. The slums, which is a pejorative word in the West, is actually not something that you think of like that in India at all. It's a geographical definition there more than it being a value judgment on people.

TOC: Can we talk a little bit about visual style? One of the things I found very striking in watching this movie is it's exuberant. Something that you do in this film that I'm particularly struck by is the balance between being close in and then stepping back and saying . . . sometimes quite literally moving back away from the action to a satellite shot of the neighborhood.

Boyle: That's just . . . because it's very difficult to get permission to go up in a helicopter in Mumbai, especially for Westerners because they're very neurotic about military stuff. When we'd fly in, if you fly in over the city as you do sometimes, visually you just want to convey to people that look or image.

TOC: The scale.

Boyle: Yeah, that scale of it. Also I just want to convey the way that wherever people are working they grow these slums. Say they are building a tower, like a Trump Tower [gestures out window at Trump Tower]. Around the bottom of it would be this phenomenal city just built by the guys who build the Trump Tower. Then what happens of course is that Trump authorities can get rid of those slums or try to, but they come back again and they'll just regroup again.

In fact there is this thing in India where you don't try and bully people into your way of life. You accept that's the way it is. It's this fatalism thing they have. We regard fatalism as quite negative. I don't think they see it like that. It's quite a positive thing there and in a funny kind of way, it's quite liberating. It's a very odd sensation that you feel there. The fact that your life is set for you by fate is actually—you think it's terrible because you wouldn't do anything then, would you? The fact is that it doesn't work like that. It's actually amazingly freeing as well. Anyway, sorry I didn't really answer that question.

TOC: No, it's wonderful stuff, but maybe I'll just push a little further. It seems to me like one of the big challenges when you approach this script is that you're telling a story that covers years. There are certain kinds of things you have to do for us viewers.

Boyle: At first we did that lazy thing that you always do; "when it's this period, why don't we have it look like this." It's basically kind of fifteen years ago, eight years ago, and now. Then I thought, I don't want to do that and I don't want them to feel like flashbacks. I want you to feel each thing that you are looking at; even though it was thirteen years ago that it happened, you're actually feeling like it's just now. I didn't want it to feel like a period thing.

That was a good decision because when we got to editing we went back and forward much more fluidly than I thought we would. You go back just for one line and then come back into present time without saying "here is a flashback." So there is no [makes dramatic whoosh sound] on the soundtrack. There is none of that. You just want it to be fluid, like memory. Like the way you smell something and you have a vivid memory of the smell. It's so intense. We tried to capture that, so what we focused on was flexibility in terms of being able to visually capture the incredible changeability of the place, you know. You've got to be aware and responsive to that.

So we came up with this digital system, 70 percent of the film is shot on it, which is incredibly lightweight. It allows the cameraman to strap the hard drive to his back and carry a thing about that size [gestures to suggest a box about eight inches on each side] which is the camera lens with a gyro on it. You can separate it from the body and you can strap it to a crane if you want that. But you can also use it very flexibly. The people are an issue because there are thousands of them and they all want to watch what you are doing. They don't quite see it as a proper film. They sort of go, "oh this isn't a proper film."

TOC: Because there's not a guy with a big, conventional camera, right?

Boyle: They get pissed off and that's the big benefit. Those were the things that dictated it more than like period, more than saying this is the period, this is the next period, and this is now. We try to be very fluid across all the periods. The kids are different, obviously, and that's enough for you to be getting on with.

TOC: Yeah, to mark the time, it's much easier. Probably much easier than if we had someone who was twenty, thirty, and forty where we have to think "Oh, well he's got a big bushy Afro, oh it's the seventies."

Boyle: I know. It was very interesting. I was very liberated by the whole experience. They had to drag me away in the end, which is always a good sign. It's very frustrating at the time because you think, "Why are we stopping? I thought they said we were going to go on with this forever." It's very frustrating then but I actually realize it's a very good thing because I have had that before on a film. I had that on *Trainspotting*, where I was just lost in it. I just thought why can't I just keep going?

TOC: Why can't I make the film forever, right?

Boyle: I keep working on the day off. I organize the days off so I have some crew who always had days off on other days and I could go in and work with them. They had to drag me away in the end. The other thing we did is we used this very high-resolution camera which is like the stills camera, the Canon Eos camera. It takes like eleven frames a second but it shoots at like 8k resolution so you get this amazing intensity of focus in it. You can blend the images on the computer now quite simply and it feels like a source of, it's not absolutely perfect motion, but it feels real. That camera you can go anywhere with in India because nobody thinks it's a journalist or a filmmaker. We used that at the Taj Mahal, where you aren't allowed near anything, and we used that in lots of different places.

TOC: It sounds like you're really invigorated by playing down at the scrappy level. "Let's figure out what we can do with this tiny camera."

Boyle: That's what I like. That's why I like not having too much money. I mean it's a lot of money anyway; $15 million is a lot of money. But it's better than having $50 million and everyone saying you can do whatever you want. It's not that freeing ironically.

TOC: Did it take going to India to do that? You went to India. That's a huge jump.

Boyle: I guess so, but you don't . . . it's a bit of an adventure, which is exciting. One of the great things around this job is that you do occasionally go . . . it's like doing publicity, you get to go on tour around America which involves getting on another plane. It's wonderful as well; you mention to anybody on the street what you're going to do. "I'm going to go tour around America for three weeks." They go "Oh wow, can I come?"

TOC: And you're spending all day in a hotel room.

Boyle: [Laughs] Still, it's a pretty nice hotel room. So you've got the adventure of it as well. It's very exciting especially if you've got a good story. And this is a great script. You read it and it's very simple and you go "Well I'd watch that film. For fuck's sake, I'd watch that film, it's really good!"

[Publicist leans into the room.]

TOC: I sense that my time is running out, so maybe this is a good last place to go: Everybody feels this exuberant liberation at the end of the film. It's the credit sequence, with the cast dancing. I suddenly looked back on the whole film and I said "Oh this is in many ways like Indian cinema!" It mixes gangsters and moments of comedy and deep romance—but romance that is always chaste. We barely get a kiss in this movie, just like most Bollywood films. But the thing that I appreciated is that we're not clubbed over the head with it . . . were you thinking about the Bollywood tradition at all?

Boyle: All the things you said are true. As a filmmaker in India, you feel them because you're there working; you feel chaste romance as part of the culture, you feel the fact that they never kiss is part of the culture, you feel all of these things so your film in some way—and this is true for Simon as well obviously writing it—reflects that because you're try-ing to live in a culture and you're trying to set the story in a culture that is realistic and believable and that you're respectful to.

I think the chaste nature of the love story also adds to the exuber-ance of storytelling because you compensate for it by this breathless-ness. The breathlessness of not consummating the action. The thing about the dance is . . . I knew we were going to have a dance because you work there for eight months, you can't not dance. If you live and work in Mumbai, you're going to dance. That feels like a much more honest way to approach it than to think about doing something clever. You want to end the film like it's been the whole eight months for you making it. So it felt really natural and as soon as we started doing it, we just thought yeah . . . And everybody dances there. It's no problem. Dev [Patel, the male lead] didn't dance because he is from London. He was a bit embarrassed. Freida Pinto [the female lead] helped him a lot actually. She's not a dancer, but she can dance. They just love her. It's as simple as people going to a movie and singing a song that's a hit in a movie. You just sing a song. I think it's because it's such a physical experience. There are so many people that the chance to move people a couple of feet away from you and just dance is really valuable.

TOC: It's organized though. That's the part that's so interesting. In a film in which people bumping against people is chaos for much of the film, our visions of the slums is navigations through a chaos of people. The thing about the dance is that it's a huge number of people in that train station, but it's incredibly coordinated.

Boyle: There are patterns in India, and you just have to be open to find them really. You cannot seek them in an aggressive or possessive way. You have to just be open to them. At first it appears to be com-pletely chaotic, but they have to find a way of living with each other. Occasionally this violence—usually set up by extreme religious fanat-ics—inspires the crowd in a bad way but most of the time they do live together. Somehow, it organizes itself, but it won't reveal the pattern to you. Occasionally you will benefit from the pattern but you'll never really fully understand it and nor should you try.

Slumdog Millionaire:
Danny Boyle Interview

Catherine Bray/2008

From catherinebray.wordpress.com. Originally published in *4Talent* magazine in December 2008. Reprinted with permission.

Not that many interviews begin with a globally respected film director spontaneously reassuring their interviewer regarding the current state of the economy. And not too many interviews also incorporate a debate on how and where the women of Indian slums manage to dispose of their excrement in such total secrecy compared to their unabashed menfolk, who think nothing of shitting in the street. But then Danny Boyle, comfortably placed within Britain's top five finest living directors for the best part of a decade, isn't someone you would ever call a predictable interviewee.

"You'll be fine," he assures me, having opened the conversation with small talk about the dire state of the economy. "How old are you? Oh, you'll be fine. I remember there was a crisis the first time we bought a proper house. We bought it at the top of the property boom for £189,000, and literally the next week the market crashed and it was suddenly worth, like, £114,000, and it was negative equity. Awful." As ever with Danny, the world of film is never more than a sentence away, and true to form he segues swiftly into reminiscence: "I remember meeting Anthony Minghella at the time—late eighties, early nineties, just after this crash—and he said, 'Don't worry about it; you'll be fine.' He was right."

Economy dealt with, time to tackle the really big issues. Time to talk crap, literally. The reason Danny has shite firmly on the brain when we meet for an hour's chat at the Hospital Club in Covent Garden is that his latest film, *Slumdog Millionaire*, is partly set precisely where the name might suggest: the slums of Mumbai. Where, Danny is keen to convey: "You do get shit all over you. There's nowhere to shit; people shit everywhere. Although you never see the women shitting. I was there a year, on and off, and for eight months full-time. You see men doing it all the time. Men and boys. All the time—and you have to get your head around that. But you never see women." He pauses to allow the mystery to fully sink in. "There were all these rumors: 'Oh, they get up in the night'—but I was up in the night, and I never saw them. There are these little plastic bags everywhere, tied up very neatly. It must be that; that's the only logical explanation."

You'll hear many directors pontificate about getting their hands dirty and bonding as a team, but most of them don't have contending with the open toilets of Mumbai in mind. Yet without sounding pretentious, Danny manages to turn talk of the most ignoble of circumstances into a subtle point about a working system in which, despite the inherently hierarchical nature of feature film production, basic equalities are acknowledged. "You can't get all squeamish about it. We all do it; we've just got a very elaborate way of disposing of it over here. It happened to most of us there—it didn't happen to me, I was very lucky—but it happened that most of us were caught short at some point."

"Your British crew are mortified that they've just had to go in front of you, but there's nowhere to go. Your Indian crew just look at you and shrug. I remember Thomas the gaffer being caught short; we were on this little island, nothing there. But it was kind of liberating, because we're so guarded, so private, about that sort of thing in the West, and yet we all do it."

Whether down to the defecatory egalitarianism of its crew or not, one of the great things about *Slumdog Millionaire* is that although it successfully holds a magnifying glass to the underbelly of India's slums, it doesn't patronize its subject, or seek to suggest that just because your street is your toilet that your life must likewise be a pile of crap. Like Charles Dickens did well over a century before, writer Simon Beaufoy [*The Full Monty*] captures in his script for *Slumdog Millionaire* something of the haphazard, teeming reality of an enormous hive of a city in flux, changing faster than it has at probably any other point in its history. Within that setting, our good-hearted hero, Jamal [Dev Patel, *Skins*], suffers the slings and arrows that come with a truly outrageous fortune, as he tries to win the woman he loves—if that means going on *Who Wants to Be a Millionaire*, so be it.

Danny concurs wholeheartedly with the idea that despite the modern trappings, there's a Dickensian vibe at work here. "It's classic storytelling, isn't it? The first thing Simon said to me after I read the script and we met was, 'It's Dickens. It's classic Dickens.' You can't avoid the shadow of Dickens. It's absolute fable. Highs and lows, slight hysteria, convenience, coincidence, good brother, bad brother, impossibly beautiful and unattainable girl taken away whenever you get close."

Perhaps slightly wired on the strong coffee we're drinking, Danny talks fast and fluently on this topic; clearly a subject that's dear to him. "We've lost that in the West; we've exiled the extreme stuff to fantasy and superhero movies. The stuff that's left is very cerebral, quite dry, serious drama. Maybe a bit of child abuse thrown in, to pep things up. But for this film, Simon embraced this rich, architectured style of Dickensian writing." Although the fate-led storytelling itself presents an enjoyably vivid, heightened reality in which plausibility is left by the wayside, the backdrop against which Simon and Danny's narrative plays out—and the cities they capture so strongly—feel 100 percent true to life. That's probably because unlike, say, Wes Anderson (whose 2008 film *The Darjeeling Limited* features some of the most nauseatingly glib, depressingly crass, and fundamentally dishonest depictions of India ever committed to film), Danny Boyle headed east aiming to capture something of what was really out there, and not simply to depict what was in his head before he went. Coming with a pre-packaged notion of an entire continent, as some directors do, is rarely the best approach in film-making, and it's not something local crews warm to either, Danny found.

"They're funny: the Indian crews say to you, 'Ah, there'll be cows in your movie, yeah?' and they're taking the piss, because they expect a Westerner to turn up and make it all about shots of sacred cows and all that stuff. So we tried to avoid that," Danny laughs. "There are a couple of cows in it actually, but they're incidental cows; you couldn't avoid them. But you don't try to crowbar them in. You can't come with your film pre-made. Obviously you've got your scripts, but you're genuinely open to change."

A rapport with an Indian crew established, Danny credits his Indian co-director Loveleen Tandan with helping him avoid other cultural dangers. "She started out as casting director, but helped me in every way it's possible to imagine. You need that; you need somebody who's got the confidence to tell the director they're wrong, which a lot of people lack. People just want a quiet life. Culturally, she would tell me if I was wrong about things."

At this point I raise the specter of Woody Allen's later London films. "That's the problem! Especially with legends. Who's going to tell a legend, 'Doesn't happen like that, love?' They just go, 'Sure Woody, fantastic." Co-directing with a large local team in a fast-moving foreign country involves a degree of trust and collaboration not often associated with the archetypal lone auteur, an image that still hangs over what we feel great direction might look like. But would a perfectionist, Kubrickean style of film-making ever have worked on a film like this? "It isn't a controlled environment, but I think Kubrick would have responded to it. It does make you rethink the way you work straight away. If you want to control Mumbai or change it, or alter it, you might as well go home, because you're just going to waste money."

Lest we run away with the idea that *Slumdog* was filmed on the fly, guerrilla-style, Danny clarifies: "It's not documentary-type shooting. You're ambitious—you're not just recording it as-is—but you don't try to clear the street or drive it all away, you work around it. If you do try to create a controlled environment, it looks fake. We did a few scenes, and you look at it and go, 'That's not Mumbai.' And you have to dump it and start again." As he talks about Mumbai and Eastern psychological differences, it would be easy to get the impression that Danny had undergone a Lennon-esque enlightenment in India, a circumstance that—were it true—you would be right to treat with suspicion, given the slump in quality that too often follows such apparent conversions in the creative industries. This was certainly a concern for executives at Pathé and Warners when they found out that a third of their supposedly English-language film could now be lost in translation. Danny remembers an awkward phone-call. "I had to ring Warners and Pathé and tell them a third of the film would now be in Hindi with subtitles. And the silence, Catherine, when I said that. The silence on the other end of the phone . . . I was in this hotel room very late at night, because L.A. had just got up, and the silence, the silence!" He laughs again, recalling what one can only imagine as the excruciating tension of that moment. "You could tell they thought, 'He's gone insane. He's going to bring back a fucking yoga film about hippies and Hindi and maharishis.' That was what they really thought."

It would eventually become apparent even to studio execs that the change in language for the sections of the film involving young Indian children was the only way to go, and was not symptomatic of a moment of mistaken whimsy on the part of the director. "Obviously we'd originally sold an English film to Warners and Pathé. But we got out there and started auditions, and of course the only kids that speak English at seven—and even then not very well—are the middle-class kids. Very highly educated kids. And they were so wrong."

It wasn't all about their speech: the childhood obesity issue is not confined to Britain. "They've got a fast-food problem in India, and the middle-class kids look chubby. I'd be going location scouting with Loveleen around the slums in the afternoons, and the kids look completely different. They're skinny, they're lithe—they're survivors." Trusted advisor Loveleen stepped up to the plate at this point and convinced Danny that the portions of the script covering our hero Jamal's childhood would have to be filmed in Hindi. "So I did it. That's the joy of not taking too much money. You can take unilateral decisions like that and just say, 'Translate it.' We did it and it came alive. The film took off—whoof!—like that."

I hazard a guess that another major factor in *Slumdog Millionaire's* artistic success is that Danny is back in his element: filming in a big city. I trail off mid-sentence, searching for an agreeable way to end a thought that began: "You film cities so well, better than . . ." Danny steps in to spare me the embarrassment: "Better than I do other stuff. I can certainly say that. I certainly feel at home. I like nature within the city, but I just don't get on with the ski-slopes or the beaches or the countryside. They're fine for a day, two days maximum, but then it's just, 'Where are the people?' Give me the people!"

Indeed, in its frenetic, affectionate story of an underdog struggling against odds stacked high against him in a big city, surrounded by urban contempt for his 'loser' status, *Slumdog* summons Danny's first major breakthrough, *Trainspotting*, irresistibly to mind. And of course there's *Slumdog's* soon-to-be infamous toilet-diving scene, something Danny is acutely aware will draw comparisons with the earlier film. "I was aware of the toilet when we were doing it, and it's one of the few times when I was really, really aware—'I've been here before'—and normally, if you ever have an instinct like that, you change the scene so you've not been there before. But it was such a good scene, we had to leave it in." We're back to that British obsession again: "We're obsessed with toilets. We're British. You see hundreds of films abroad; you won't see a toilet in any of them."

Slumdog Millionaire's successful mixing of the spirit of Mumbai, of slum kids, Hindi, and a country in fast-forward, with British touchstones of Dickensian storytelling, quiz-shows, and toilets, anchored successfully by the performance of *Skins'* Dev Patel in a breakout lead role, should strike a chord with a national and international audience.

Crucially, it's a film that it's difficult to imagine being made in any other way, by any other director. Balancing his healthy respect for his own instincts—and those of his trusted advisers—with a practical awareness of studios' cash-flow fears seems to be a hallmark of Danny's working methods. It's something he illustrates with a story about the difficulties of marrying the ideals of a script with the realities of filming. "You have to get permission to film everywhere," he laments as he discusses the film's various locations. "We ran that side of it like a parallel universe to the film. The bureaucracy, the rubber-stamping, this stuff that takes an eternity, sometimes years—that was run entirely separately as far as possible. You try not to let it affect you as you film; if it did you'd never get the film made. We'd still be there."

"So the guys apply for what we wanted, and we'd be filming, not thinking about this whole parallel universe, and generally being quite light-hearted about the process." But when it came to filming at the Taj Mahal, compromise was needed as the ocean of bureaucracy collided with the directorial vision, and the practicalities of interacting with a different culture. The Taj Mahal and surrounding area is run entirely on the income generated by the tourism at the Taj, overseen by what Danny describes as a "sort of mafia really: photographers, tour-guides, you know. It's quite sophisticated. They saw us turn up with these kids, and gradually they realized what we were up to and got annoyed. Very annoyed. They got heavy at one point, and we got chased out."

"The parallel universe guys realized we had a problem, packed our bags and drove us out of there at high speed. We weren't really finished, but had to cross the state border before they injuncted the film, which could trap it in the courts for five years. Five years waiting for them to release the film, imagine."

Knowing how to pick your battles, when to persist doggedly, and whose advice to trust are clearly key skills for anyone hoping to juggle executive expectations linked to huge sums of money with, on the other hand, the subtler concerns of good storytelling that are the reason you're filming in the first place. It's surely no coincidence that Danny found himself drawn to a script in which just such a juggling act is played out. The film's hero Jamal meets an endless stream of compromises and short-term setbacks, but never backs down in the long-term pursuit of his ultimate goal. Even when interrogated by the powers that be as to just what exactly he thinks he's playing at.

Interview: Danny Boyle on *Slumdog Millionaire*

Ambrose Heron/2009

From FILMdetail.com, January 8, 2009. Reprinted with permission. Transcribed by Brent Dunham.

FD: *Slumdog Millionaire* is a new movie that's out this week and we're joined by the director, Danny Boyle. Danny, thanks for being here today.

DB: Pleasure. Thanks for having us.

FD: Okay, now, I last spoke to you when *Sunshine* came out and you told me your next film was going to be about a kid on the Hindi version of *Who Wants to Be a Millionaire* and it was only afterwards that I thought, "What's that going to be? Is he doing a Bollywood movie? What's going on?" And I saw the film at the London Film Festival and I was really blown away by it and it all kind of made sense but, for people coming new to the film this weekend on its U.K. release, tell us a bit about the story and how you got attached to the project.

DB: Well, it's got this fantastic premise: it's about a slum kid, the "slumdog" of the title, and he goes on the Indian version of *Who Wants to Be a Millionaire*. And it is the biggest cash prize in the world, relative to the standard of living. I mean it's an enormous amount of money that's offered, dangled in front of a very poor country, and he starts to answer all these questions and he gets every single question right, to his astonishment, and to theirs. So much so that they, actually, before the final question, they take him away and try and torture him into confession that he's cheated because they imagine he's just tried to hijack the money. He has not, in fact. In fact, the reason he's on the show has nothing to do with the money, it's to do with something else entirely, which is he's got this girl who he has loved and lost in this

145

chaos of Mumbai and all he knows is that she watches this show. And he figures if he gets on the show and stays in the chair long enough, she'll see him and they can get back together again. So, that's actually a very pure reason, at the heart of it, which has nothing to do with finance, to do with money, to do with the glamour, the glory, the fame of television, you know?

FD: It's a fascinating film to watch because there's so many different elements to it. Let's start off with the script, which is adapted from a novel called Q &A by Simon Beaufoy, who most people might know wrote *The Full Monty*. It's a wonderful jigsaw puzzle of a script that criss-crosses between different timeframes, and the first ten minutes of this movie, I was like, "Whoa. What's going on here?" Because we see the main kid of the title, who is played by Dev Patel, but we also see him earlier in his life. Was that always the intention to sort of move around these different time zones?

DB: It's got this wonderful fluid sense of time, so they are effectively flashbacks but you don't feel like you're watching a flashback movie. It feels like *The Usual Suspects* in the sense that, although it's a different tone, it just goes backward and foreword in time, and yet it's not confusing because you have different actors playing him at different—so you know exactly where you are with the different kids. But it's just backward and foreword and it's all inter-mingled in the way that memories are and bits of his life, which have been tragic to live through, suddenly become useful to him. All the horror he's been through suddenly allows him to answer a question really easily. And the guys can't believe—it's an impossible question, they're designed to be impossible to answer but he can answer it, you know? And it gives him the next step on his quest to get closer and closer to this girl.

FD: And it weaves wonderfully with the format of the show we should say. But, also, the other thing that's really striking about the film is the visuals. Now, you capture the chaos of Mumbai, the poverty, but also the joy the characters have in their lives. Was that another intention to create this widescreen, full-on journey, if you like?

DB: It's maximum city, that city. Everything's maximum. The horror that you see, and you do see some terrible things in it, but the sense of joy, the sense of dedication to life being lived at its fullest is irresistible. And people say it's got a kind of "feel good ending," and that's very useful to put in a film, isn't it? And I guess it is, of course, but the truth is that isn't why we ended it like that. We ended it like that because that's the way the city demands you end a film about that city. Because, however imperfectly, it's dedicated to happiness, that city. As a combination of business and pleasure: business, everybody's doing deals, pleasure, everybody loves dance, music, Bollywood, the movies. And, when you come into it, this effervescence is created, which lifts you out of some of the horror that is there. It's an exhilarating place to make a film and you want to bring that sense back with you. That was what we wanted to try and do with the film.

FD: Yeah, and tell us a bit more about the visuals of this film, the cinematographer is Anthony Dod Mantle who has shot some Dogme films.

DB: Yes, he has.

FD: He actually lives in Denmark, doesn't he? And tell us about this new digital camera you used. Because there are some scenes in the film where I guess you couldn't have gone in with a big rig of a camera. Tell us about the camera you used in certain scenes in the film.

DB: Well, I've worked with Anthony a few times. He's British but he lives in Denmark now and he's worked with Dogme and he's the leading digital cameraman in the world, really. Although, he would personally prefer to work on film, I think. But he is brilliant at his digital camera work and I love the digital cameras because they're more flexible than film cameras. And they're beginning, of course, now to produce results which are as—the quality is as good as film, anyway. But the advantage you get is that people don't think you're filming with them because they can't quite take it seriously, especially out there. They shoot movies with big 35mm cameras, quite old and quite cumbersome cameras. But using this little equipment allowed us to move almost without people realizing what we were doing sometimes, but [it] also gives the ability to work in small spaces, to work very dynamically. And, also, you've got to think, you're talking about seven-year-old kids who are tiny, you know? They're tiny and small. You've got these great, big, hulking cameras and they're nearly as tall as these film cameras. What you want is a kind of camera that allows you to—that they can carry, which we allowed them to do at some times. And it gives you a wonderful immediacy, you know? It gets you right there somehow; there's something wonderful about it in that way. India, Mumbai, visually is extraordinary and, if you do it in the right way—you don't need to stop and look at the city, like a tourist, because, in fact, the kid, who the story is based on, is born and brought up there and he's not going to stand looking at it. He just takes it for granted in a way, so we tried to take it for granted. But you accumulate the city in the background. The whole time you're picking it up and, because you can use these cameras, the city sometimes doesn't even know you're working. So you get it for free, really.

FD: What's wonderful about the film also is that the level of the acting is just great, and I think there's a perception about Bollywood that it's all a bit cheesy, and some of it is, but there are some Indian actors here—I mean, the leads are great, the smaller kids are wonderful, the host is absolutely fantastic—but tell us about some of the Indian actors you used.

DB: He's a major actor in Bollywood. He's a massive star. He's not as big as he used to be but he is massive. He's called Anil Kapoor and he's a brilliant actor. Now he knows his acting is normally a bit "cheesy" as you say yourself, he'd admit that, because they say that's the style, that's what the audience wants. But to do "cheesy," you've got to be able to do the other stuff as well, basically, when you're a good actor, and he can do that kind of stuff. He would say, "Just make sure I'm not over the top, will you?" And I like quite like him "over the top" anyway because, like I said, everything is maximum over there. That's where the acting style comes out of. It's a big, vibrant city and, if you want to make your mark on it, you've got to speak loudly, you know? So, it tends to be quite big, the style, and I love that in the film. Sometimes it would be over the top and I would bring it down for our tastes, I suppose, but there's a huge talent there. You have a thousand films that are made a year in that one city alone and, when you've got that kind of work going on, people are going to be confident about the world they work in. Because it's not like they're out of work all year, they make a lot of films. So, they have a kind of confidence and if you measure and take some of the edge off of the style sometimes, some of the style they use in their films, you're going to get a lot of very bold, confident acting to our tastes, which is very palatable.

FD: Yeah, the story is incredible in the film but it's also an interesting story how this film got made. Tell us a bit about the financing, the whole business with the American partner/distributor, Warner Independent, which, kind of, went under as you were shooting or had shot it. And, now, it's got almost a fairytale ending with a great reaction in America. Tell us a bit about the business of getting it financed and made.

DB: It's bizarre how it kind of mirrors the journey of the kid himself.
FD: It does.
DB: It's just very, very strange. So, we raised the money based, I think probably, on the prospect of Simon Beaufoy, the writer of *The Full Monty*, doing *Who Wants to Be a Millionaire* and me as director having had a couple of successes. So, we raised $13 million. We raised $8 million of it in Europe, through this company, Pathé, and $5 million of it through this company in America, Warner Independent, a subdivision of Warner Bros. After we had made the film, using that money, Warner Bros. closed down Warner Independent as being non-economic. So we were kind of like fatherless because Warner Bros. wouldn't release this kind of film. Basically, we were a DVD, we were going to be a DVD until Fox Searchlight who are a division of Twentieth Century Fox saw the film and saw the potential for it, which is the visionary bit, I guess, because no one else could see how it would work in America. And they saw that it was basically *Rocky*: it's the story of the underdog who can do it. All the odds are against him but he can do it, and, at its heart, it's not about success or money, it's about love. And they saw that and they took it over and they're playing it. It's been in the cinemas for nine weeks, it's done over $30 million and it's absolutely extraordinary. They're buzzing about it; we've got four Golden Globe nominations and there's all this Oscar buzz on it. Now, whether we ever get any prizes or not, in a way it would be wonderful, but is irrelevant because the value has already been done because it's put us in the marketplace. It's given us a profile, it's lifted us out of this anonymity because there's no stars the West would recognize in it and it's placed it on this platform along with Brad Pitt and Sean Penn, and he's up there discussed in every kind of sentence. It's extraordinary the way—and that's the dream come true, isn't it? That's the fairytale ending: for a kid, Jamal, Dev Patel from London, just this ordinary kid whose got a small part in *Skins* and suddenly he's talked about with Sean Penn and Brad Pitt!
FD: As they say in the movie, "It was written," Danny. It's obviously difficult to get films like this financed and, when you see it, you kind of think, "Well, why aren't there more movies financed on a lower level?" Is that a problem with the film business? Too much money spent fullstop and there's not as many risks taken with lower budgets maybe?
DB: There's going to be a lot more lower-budget films made now, although everybody's always talked about that, "because there's a chance then to make a bigger profit, blah, blah." Now, it's a necessity because

the current economic times affect film just as much as they affect everybody else's life. There will still be huge films made like *The Dark Knight*, with staggering budgets, with unbelievable wealth and resources and money and success almost guaranteed, but there will also be a lot more lower-budget films made, there has to be really because there just won't be the money around to finance. And we're going to have to learn, as an industry, to work for less money, really, and nobody should cry for us either because we're well-paid as it is and times are tough for everybody. So, it will be something that can create a wave of opportunity for people as well, for younger filmmakers to come through. They don't expect big money, they don't expect big resources, but they got a story to tell.

FD: Sure. Well, *Slumdog Millionaire* is one of my favorites of this year. I think it's going to be a film that gets a lot of good word-of-mouth from audiences and it's fantastic that U.K. audiences finally get to see it this week. Danny, thanks for your time.

DB: Thanks, Ambrose.

Danny Boyle

Tavis Smiley/2009

From "Tavis Smiley" courtesy KCET/Hollywood and TS Media, Inc. January 30, 2009.

Tavis: Danny Boyle is a talented filmmaker whose resume includes acclaimed films like *Trainspotting* and *28 Days Later.* His latest is easily the most talked-about film of the year, *Slumdog Millionaire.* The movie has already won a slew of awards and is up for ten—count them, ten— Oscars including Best Picture and Best Director. Here now a scene from *Slumdog Millionaire.*

[clip played]

Tavis: So I'm sitting here watching this clip with Danny Boyle and there are two things that get my attention as we're watching this clip together. In no particular order, number one, he whispers to me thanking me for picking a different clip. As a director, you notice that people keep playing the same clips?

Danny Boyle: Yeah. It's inevitable, really, yeah. So it's nice to see a different one there.

Tavis: What do you think of that clip we showed?

Boyle: It's great because it's a performance clip, you know. I mean, it's really Dev on that day when he says, "There was no message, there was no message, there was no message." He was really mad at me because we were fighting on that day about how to do it. He's only eighteen, but he was like—you know, he had his take on how to do it and we were battling and that was the frustration that came out in that scene.

It was really good actually. I was shocked when it happened. And if you watch it, it's slightly out of focus because nobody was expecting it, you know. But we left it in because you can't repeat those things. They just happen.

Tavis: I was about to say, as a director, there are things that happen, there are things that you see that may not be technically correct, but you know when to hold on to something.

Boyle: You get that buzz. It's incredible. You think there's the film right there. You know, you get those odd moments. So much of it's technical, sometimes uncontrolled and all that kind of stuff, but it's extraordinary working in Mumbai because it's a very difficult city to control. It's so busy and you have to let go a lot, and I let go on the film a lot more than I have done on previous stuff I've done.

Tavis: Eighteen million people, it's kind of hard to hold on.

Boyle: It's like unbelievable, that amount of people. We wanted them all to be in the film and a lot of them are in the film and, thankfully, they don't have release forms there yet, so you don't have to get them all to sign (laughter).

Tavis: (Laughter) That's an inside Hollywood joke. You hate those release forms for everybody on the film. The other thing that occurred to me that got my attention as we were watching that clip a moment ago and you just expressed it, you know the dialog in this film. You know everybody's dialog or you just happen to know that scene? You were saying the words along with the actors.

Boyle: Yeah, you know the dialog. You've got it inside your head and you're kind of living the film in your head, and that's how you can help the actors sometimes if they're a bit lost on something because you have a version of it running through your head.

But you should never give them line readings, you know. That's the worst thing. But you try and express what you're after in a scene, and they have to find their way to that or, you know, they fight a bit with you. They have a different take on it. Often they're right because they're interesting actors.

They often don't look at the whole film. They often say, "Oh, I just read my part" (laughter) and you think, "How can you do that?" But, of course, it gives them an incredible perspective because their character may not know some of the other characters in the film, so it's quite good in a way that they don't know the peoples' worlds, but they know their world in an intense way.

You look at Mickey Rourke's performance in *The Wrestler* and he knows that guy from the inside, you know. When you find that kind of acting, it's mesmerizing, really special. You know, no matter what the budget is or what the circumstances you're watching it in.

Tavis: I'll come back to the movie in just a second, but since you were nominated—by the way, congratulations, Best Director nomination.

Boyle: Thank you very much.

Tavis: And all the other nine for the film. But where the Best Director nomination is concerned, I want to get to your processes if I can for a moment. You were talking a moment ago about actors and sometimes they are right because they have a sense for their own part even if they haven't read the entire script.

What's your give and take? How do you establish a relationship with the actor? When you're now an Academy-nominated director, how do you know where that zone is, where that give-and-take relationship should be or not be with the actors?

Boyle: I always try to make sure everybody can—no matter what they think of me or what their age—like Dev and most of the cast in this film are very young and inexperienced. But I always try and make sure they can all speak their mind, you know, about what they think. I have the right, in a way, to overrule them if necessary, but it's really important for me to know what they're thinking because so much is revealed by their focus on their parts, you know, by their take on it.

They always say—it's one of the things they teach you as a director—actors get you out of corners. You know, when you paint yourself into a corner and there's no time left and there's no money left, they can just get you out of a corner like that because it's kind of free. Just put the camera on them and they can take you somewhere and keep you there and transform, you know, your corner into a palace, you know.

Tavis: While we're talking about your directing, what is it like to direct a film that has received so much acclaim and, by your own admission, most of these folks aren't that experienced as thespians as yet?

Boyle: Certainly the younger characters aren't. We have a couple of guys in it, like Anil Kapoor is a big star. He's a game show host. He's a big star in India, big in Bollywood. I loved working with them all, you know. It was that mixture of experience and inexperience. It's really exciting for a director, you know, because—especially young actors. They don't bring any baggage.

I think sometimes older actors are a bit frightened of how pure they are. If they know what a scene's about and they say a line, there's nothing of "Is this making me look good? Is this making me look bad? Will people like my character more or less?" None of that. There's no business stuff involved. It's just like the line, the scene.

Tavis: "This is not in my contract, Danny! This is not in my deal!" (Laughter)

Boyle: Exactly. You don't get any of that (laughter).

Tavis: To the film itself, for those who haven't seen it, what's the story? You mentioned, of course, the talk show host. Give me the quick story line for those who haven't seen it. I have some questions I want to ask you about.

Boyle: So it's about this kid from the slums of Mumbai and he goes on the biggest game show in the world, *Who Wants to Be a Millionaire* in India. Its audience and the prize that they offer relative to living standards there is the biggest. It's the biggest game show in the world. He goes on it and he starts to answer the questions and he gets them all right.

The questions in India are very tough after the first couple of easy ones and everybody doubts him. Everybody thinks he's cheating. There must be a coughing or an accomplice in the audience or he must have a microchip hidden under his skin because there's no way he can answer these questions.

What you see in the film is—I mean, he's astonished they're asking because some of the adversities, some of the things that have happened to him in his life, allow him access to information, to knowledge, that they're asking about, so he starts to get all the questions right. Eventually, they take him off the show before the final $20 million question. They take him off the show and hand him over to the police to find out how he's cheating. You know, it's become a big nationwide thing.

In fact, he's got a completely other agenda for being on the show. It's nothing to do with the money, it's nothing to do with success or television or fame or glamour. The girl that he loves and has lost in the chaos of this city, all he knows is she watches this show and he figures, if he gets on it and stays in the chair for long enough, she'll see him and they can reconnect. So it's got a love story at its heart, you know.

Tavis: I was fascinated and maybe I'm reading too deep into this. But I was fascinated by how, to your point, he isn't cheating, but he's being asked questions and, just based upon his own life experiences, he's going back into his own—he's going inside to help answer these questions.

Maybe I'm too deep into this, but I was thinking what a wonderful metaphor for how to deal with the hard challenges, questions, issues life throws at us when we can go inside sometimes. The answers are there.

Boyle: Yeah, the answers are there.

Tavis: Am I in too deep?

Boyle: Nope. I got to say, Tavis, you're where you should be really because not a lot of people say that, but it's true actually because that's one of the kind of ideas in the film that's hidden in there. You know, he comes out of nowhere. He's not very educated. He doesn't have much going for him, but he's got a very, very rich life story and all the people who've gotten him there, good and bad people, have lots of answers for him and the challenges he's facing in his life.

I think that's a lesson for everybody really. You know, all our stories, no matter where we come from, have enormous value and sometimes we don't think they do, but they do, you know.

Tavis: I hope you'll indulge me on this, but I was doing some research on this. I'm always amazed by the back story. I mean, part of being for me a talk show host, the best thing, the most fun thing about talking to people like you is getting beyond the obvious stuff that everybody knows and just stuff that I just was unaware of. I had no idea that this thing almost went straight to DVD.

Boyle: I know.

Tavis: Tell me the back story. I mean, you got a movie that's the most talked-about film, got ten Academy Award nominations, and the thing almost didn't get to the theaters. It almost went straight to DVD.

Boyle: I know. It's been an extraordinary kind of fairy tale, the journey of the film itself when we seemed to have lost. Basically what happened is that Warner Bros. had closed their independent division, Warner Independents, for lots and lots of reasons, nothing to do with our film.

But it meant that we didn't have a specialist distributor because Warner has obviously released huge films like *Dark Knight* and *Matrix* and these huge movies. So we had to try and find another distributor. Warner, to give them their credit, they did the right thing in the end. They showed the film to Fox Searchlight.

I think it would have been a lot easier for them to do the wrong thing and it could have disappeared, but they showed it to Fox Searchlight who I'd worked with before and who are brilliant at releasing this kind of film that needs to be nurtured slowly to begin with. Fox Searchlight went mad for it and they asked us to get it ready very quickly so we could put it in the Telluride and Toronto Film Festivals where it began to get public acclaim. That's what's extraordinary about it is its word of mouth that's helped the movie.

We've had lots of wonderful critical response to it, but it's people talking to each other about it, because there's lots of barriers to an audience. A third of the film is in Hindi with subtitles, exciting subtitles, but subtitles, and it's set in India. It's on the other side of the world and it doesn't have any recognizable or conventional stars in it, and yet the heart of the story really touches people, I think.

Tavis: What made you think—I was gonna come to that, so I'm glad you went there, Danny—what made you think with all those barriers, all those potential obstacles, that the thing could play and play this well?

Boyle: I didn't know, to be honest, until I saw it in front of an American audience at Telluride and then at Toronto. You realize basically it's the *Rocky* story, you know. It's rooting for a guy who has nothing, comes out of nowhere, but he's got this dream and he gets there. Against all the odds, he gets there because of his own worth, his own internal worth, what you were saying, about himself, his own story. He can get there.

I was astonished. It was like an epiphany for me seeing it in front of an American audience rooting for him. I thought, "What's that come out of?" It's the *Rocky* story because, in the end, it's not about the money, although it's very nice that he gets it—oh, I'm giving it away there.

It's about this girl. It's a love story in the end, about the girl that he's loved all his life and he wants to rescue her from the terrible situation that she's in. He manages to via hijacking the biggest game show in the world, you know (laughter).

Tavis: I'm gonna grind an ax here for just a second, but I promise I'll get off my soapbox in a moment because I want to hear your take on this. It's fascinating to me to talk to one who's nominated as Best Director for the Academy Award.

But you mentioned a word a moment ago, humanity, and I'm always blown away by how we continue to have these debates or conversations and, quite frankly, not enough of it in this town about people of color being given opportunities in this business. My sense has always been that it doesn't matter what color they are, what part of the world they live in. If you have a story that shows the humanity of the character, it can work.

Boyle: Yeah.

Tavis: It can work. They're not all gonna be nominated for ten Academy Awards, but it's about getting to the humanity of the character and that conversation, to me, ought to supersede conversations about why we don't have African Americans and why we don't have Latinos and people in India.

This made me think about that because you hit the nail on the head. What makes the picture work is the humanity, and I don't know why Hollywood can't get that lesson. If you put people of color on, you show their humanity, their complexity of character, you make them multi-dimensional, it can work.

Boyle: I don't have to tell you this. You know this. The world is changing now anyway, you know. You can feel it changing. We've benefited from it enormously, you know. The communications have become so instant, you know, the Internet and everything. There's so much going on in the world now. The world is a smaller place and we know it's an incredibly rich place as well.

And these stories, everybody's story, deserves to be told. As an industry and I'm part of it, that's our responsibility, to tell everybody's story, you know. They're not all gonna, you know, have the acclaim, but they all deserve to be told in a way. I think the victory of *Slumdog* in a way, its success, will hopefully ensure that that process, you know, really kicks off in some kind of way. It's a very special thing to be associated with.

The actors in the film got this award from the Screen Actors Guild the other night, which was extraordinary because the Screen Actors Guild obviously has thousands and thousands of actors in America, the American film industry. They reached out and gave their award, their ensemble award, to these actors who they did not know from Adam. They had no idea who they were. They're from another industry on the other side of the world. This is all so enormous. It was an overwhelming moment. It felt almost historic, you know, in entertainment terms. It was extraordinary and that is very typical of America, that reaching out, you know.

Tavis: How did the cast take—in their private moments with you, how did they take being celebrated in that way by this American industry?

Boyle: They were overcome. Anil Kapoor, who's a very, very sophisticated guy, he was overcome by it. You know, he was overwhelmed by the response (laughter). He forgot to say a few things and then Freida came in and said them for him.

I thought it was wonderful because he's been a wonderful ambassador for the film in India and, you know, around the world because there's a huge Indian audience around the world, in America and in the U.K., you know, and they've loved seeing themselves, you know, in their homelands because America is their homeland or the U.K. is their homeland.

Tavis: The flip side of that is, while you're absolutely right, the overwhelming majority of people in India, I'm told or at least read, are celebrating this. There is that slice and there always is of people who think that Mr. Boyle didn't do a good enough job, didn't have the requisite care and concern for the image of Mumbai, that it shows the country in abject poverty. Your response to that?

Boyle: It started a big debate about—poverty and the slums are a huge and very complex part of this incredible city. Normally, Bollywood doesn't really use the slums or uses it very little, so it started a big debate about whether Bollywood should use these stories more and it's wonderful to be part of that.

The privilege of working there, also, you have the responsibility of standing up and taking criticism and it's quite right that nobody's ever gonna capture it perfectly, but you try and get as much of the city included in there as possible, and that's what we tried to do.

Tavis: I'm always curious, again, to the back story here. What attracted you to this script when you saw it?

Boyle: Well, I was kind of—there's an odd moment with scripts sometimes and it's only happened to me twice. Once on *Trainspotting* and once on this one—

Tavis: —which I want to talk about in a moment, but go ahead.

Boyle: Well, I started reading it and I knew I was gonna make it. I've not gotten beyond ten or fifteen pages of the script, but I knew I was gonna do it. You look back on that and think, "That's crazy. It could have been terrible, the other ninety pages or whatever." But you get picked. They're like stray dogs that follow you home. They decide, "You are gonna be looking after me from now on." (Laughter) It's really odd, but it's true.

I think it was partly the universality of the story. I felt extraordinary the story and yet it was very particular because it's set in this extraordinary city, the vibrant city. Against all the odds, this city keeps going. It's overcrowded. There's great poverty there as well in the slums, but there's enormous breathtaking kind of resilience of the people, you know.

And this life force, this celebratory sense they have of life which is celebrated in Bollywood, in song and dance in Bollywood, but also in business. Business is being done everywhere at all different levels of society. It's extraordinary. I love cities like, you know—I mean, I went to New York when I was, you know, in the early eighties and Mumbai is like New York. It's a city that grabs you by the throat and says, "Welcome. You'll never be the same again."

Tavis: I was about to ask you, since you mention New York City, given the time that you spent in Mumbai, how does it compare to other locales that you've shot on location?

Boyle: It's extraordinary because, I mean, every city has extremes. But in Mumbai, I believe it's unique that the extremes are right beside each other. They sit right beside each other, so the slums are everywhere.

There's huge rich buildings, and they're surrounded by slums and nobody tries to separate these two extremes of life. It's true of all walks of life. They're both geographically, you know, things situated emotionally, you go through these extraordinary days where you see terrible things and then you see the most wonderful things as well.

We tried to get that sense in the film. The film, because of it, has many different tones. You know, it's funny, it's frighteningly sad and terrifying, and then it's celebratory with the dance at the end. We didn't try and make a smooth arc across those tones. We just let them bash into one another. Thankfully, it's worked. Otherwise, I wouldn't be here, you know.

Tavis: Which raises a fascinating question for me. I don't know how you would describe it, but you have a style—I'm talking about *Trainspotting* in a moment—but you have this style. I don't how to describe it, but it's like a long music video. It's fast-paced, the energy in the way you shoot. Does that make sense? I mean, you have a style that really moves.

Boyle: I love music and its influences whether there's music there or not. I love momentum in films. I have this theory. I mean, they call it the motion picture industry for a reason, I think.

Tavis: (Laughter) I get it. Motion pictures, yeah.

Boyle: When our ancestors—silent movies—the first time they watched locomotive trains pass across the screen and they screamed. There's something extraordinary about momentum in films, and there's so much kind of real time for two hours or whatever it is. You live through the story and, if you get caught up in it, you're breathless and frightened and crying and happy.

I love that sense of momentum in films and I always try to—I don't make action movies, but I try and make every movie as like an action movie as I can. That's sort of one of my principles, you know.

Tavis: You picked the right word. That's what I was looking for. Momentum, it does have momentum. Finally, since you mentioned it and I just saw it again the other night, I don't want to color the question too much, but what do you think now when you look back? Have you seen *Trainspotting* lately?

Boyle: (Laughter).

Tavis: Have you seen it lately?

Boyle: I see bits of it (laughter) all the time, different places.

Tavis: What do you think about that? That's extraordinary.

Boyle: It's just unbelievable, kind of, you know, a launching pad. It's a brilliant book it's based on, absolutely brilliant book, and you could make ten more films with that book, you know, different kind of films, approaches to it. So you should always remember where you come from and where things come from, you know, and it came from that book. The privilege of working on it, you know, it made kind of filming it easy in a funny kind of way.

Tavis: Well, great place to end on. *Trainspotting*, if you haven't seen it, you got to go check that out, first of all. But the movie I'm sure he would love for you to go see right about now (laughter) is called *Slumdog Millionaire* directed by Danny Boyle.

He is up for an Academy Award as Best Director. The film nominated for ten Academy Awards. It should be quite a night. We shall see in a matter of weeks from now for this film, *Slumdog Millionaire*, that almost went straight to DVD. Who knew? Danny Boyle, glad to have you here.

Boyle: Very nice to meet you.

Tavis: It's been nice to see you.

Director Danny Returns Home to a Rip-Roaring Welcome

Bury Times/2009

Courtesy of the *Bury Times* newspaper, Greater Manchester, U.K., March 5, 2009.

It may have been a million miles away from the bright lights of Hollywood, but film director Danny Boyle was given a rip-roaring welcome when he returned to his home town of Radcliffe.

The fifty-two-year-old, whose film *Slumdog Millionaire* won eight Oscars, was besieged by fans and autograph collectors on Sunday when he honored his promise to pop back down to St. Mary's Catholic Social Club in Pine Street.

The cheering fans and a large gathering of journalists came as a surprise for Danny. "This is amazing. You expect it when you're on the red carpet and in L.A., but you don't expect it here in Radcliffe," he said.

Among the waiting fans was seven-year-old Arwel McManamon, of Farcroft Avenue.

Danny's flying visit to Radcliffe was announced in the morning service at St. Mary and St. Philip Neri RC Church, where he was an altar boy as a child, and Arwel asked him to sign the church newsletter.

His mum, Theresa, said: "We've just come out of church and thought it would be good to meet Danny. It's nice that he hasn't forgotten where he comes from. He seems very kind and will give his time to people. I am sure his family are very proud of him."

Danny, a former pupil of St. Mary's RC Primary School, visited the club yesterday to show off his Oscar award for best director.

He enjoyed a glass of lemonade with his father, Frank, sister, Maria, and other relatives and friends, and passed around his Oscar.

He had carried the golden statue in a "non-descript blue bag"—instead of the Marks and Spencer carrier bag he had used to take his BAFTA and Golden Globe awards there two weeks earlier.

But he had to warn fellow club members to be careful with the coveted award.

He said: "It's got a bit damaged now because I have been taking it everywhere and letting people hold it. It just stays on a shelf most of the time though.

"I said if I won one of these I would buy everyone in the bar a drink. I said the same thing about winning a BAFTA and a Golden Globe. It's getting very pricey now!"

Danny may have come a long way since moving out of his childhood home in Holland Street, but it is clear that he has never forgotten his roots.

He said: "The first thing anybody said to me here when I came here with the Golden Globe and the BAFTA was, 'how the bloody hell did anyone like you win a BAFTA?' That's exactly the sort of thing you need saying."

He added: "I have always been someone who feels like they belong here, rather than in L.A. or somewhere else. I live in London because my kids are there and for work, but I get home as much as I can. I feel like I want to share this moment with everyone here."

The local boy has certainly made a name for himself after a string of hit films.

But it almost didn't happen as a young Danny dreamed of becoming either a train driver or a priest.

He said: "I wanted to be a train driver, then I was going to be a priest because my mother was very religious. I was at this college in Bolton and one of the priests said he didn't think I should do it. I am very grateful to him and always think about whether he was trying to save the priesthood or me."

After working in television and the theatre since the 1980s, Danny moved into films around fifteen years ago.

"I have been very lucky. *Trainspotting* was an enormous success and *28 Days Later* was a massive commercial success. Nothing caught fire like this though. It's uncontrollable. It's because of the timing—for some reason, in that moment, it's what everyone wants to see," he said.

Danny was so delighted with *Slumdog Millionaire*'s success—it picked up eight Oscars in total including best picture and best director—that he jumped around on the stage of the Kodak Theatre like Tigger from *Winnie the Pooh* after making a promise to his children.

He said: "I've never prepared a speech so I was thinking slightly impulsively and odd things came to mind like the Tigger thing. The real deal was that I would wear a Tigger costume and sing the Tigger song, but luckily there was a forty-five-second time limit and I got out of doing that."

The pressure is on for Danny to make another hit film hot on the heels of his current blockbuster, but he insists he has no immediate plans. However, rumors are already rife that he could be asked to direct the next James Bond film.

It has also been suggested he could appear on the celebrity version of *Who Wants to Be a Millionaire*.

"I don't know what the future holds. I will start work next week and have a think about reading and writing and what to do next. You just have to get back on the bicycle and see what happens," he said.

He has also been put forward for being given the freedom of Bury.

Danny joked: "Everyone was saying my dad will be able to graze sheep on his lawn now!"

He added: "You can get lost in the business, but I have never been like that. I have always tried to make films so that people from this town can watch them. There are no cinemas anymore in Radcliffe and people have to go to Bury or Bolton to watch them, but I always want the people who I lived with to watch my films "

He also praised Bury-based rock band Elbow, who are set to receive the "freedom" honor alongside Paralympian Zoe Robinson, from Lowercroft.

Guy Garvey lead singer from Elbow sent a message of congratulations to Danny after his Oscar success. Danny said: "I am a big fan and it's wonderful to see their success.

"My biggest influence is music. That's my biggest single influence and I'm proud to come from an area where the music scene and the rock stars it produces are unbelievable."

Danny will also take a break from his jet-setting lifestyle to return to his home in London and spend time with his children, Grace, Gabriel, and Caitlin.

Danny said: "My top moments are my kids. They top everything. That's the moment you feel real pride—when they're born and they're okay."

But he has plenty to bring him back to Radcliffe, especially after being made an honorary life member of St. Mary's Catholic Social Club.

He also hopes to make more trips to Gigg Lane to see his beloved Bury FC in action. For the life-long Shakers fan insists that winning an Oscar does not mean all his dreams have come true.

He said: "The last time we won the FA Cup was 1903 so there's still a lot to wish for!"

Index

Printed in the United States
by Baker & Taylor Publisher Services